JOSÉ MARTÍ
Major Poems

JOSÉ MARTÍ
Major Poems

A BILINGUAL EDITION

English Translation by
Elinor Randall

Edited, with an introduction, by
Philip S. Foner

HM
HOLMES & MEIER PUBLISHERS, INC.
New York · London

First published in the United States of America 1982 by
Holmes & Meier Publishers, Inc.
30 Irving Place
New York, N.Y. 10003

Great Britain:
Holmes & Meier Publishers, Ltd.
131 Trafalgar Road
Greenwich, London SE10 9TX

Designed by Paul Chevannes

Library of Congress Cataloging in Publication Data

Martí, José, 1853-1895.
  José Martí, major poems.

  English and Spanish.
  I. Randall, Elinor. II. Foner, Philip Sheldon,
1910−   III. Title.
PQ7389.M2A27   1982   861   81-20016
ISBN 0-8419-0761-7   AACR2
ISBN 0-8419-0834-6 (pbk.)

Manufactured in the United States of America

CONTENTS

INTRODUCTION

JOSÉ Julián Martí y Pérez, "The Apostle" of Cuba, was born on January 28, 1853, in a humble two-story house on Paula Street in Havana. His father, Mariano Martí y Navarro, the son of a poor ropemaker in Valencia, Spain, had come to Havana as a sergeant in the Spanish army, married a girl from Spain, Leonor Pérez y Cabera, and decided to remain in Cuba, hoping to find a better life for himself there. He obtained a transfer to the police force and served as a night watchman in Havana and other cities.

Although his father's meager resources limited his interest in his son's education, the boy's godfather agreed to pay for his studies at the Municipal School for Boys in Havana. At the age of thirteen, he entered the Colegio de San Pablo. Its director was Rafael María de Mendive, a revolutionary poet and journalist, who had dedicated himself to "furthering the advancement and improvement of the society" in which he lived. Martí continued his studies under Mendive until his teacher was imprisoned by the Spanish authorities, allegedly for attending a political rally at a local theater. A visit to his imprisoned teacher left an indelible imprint on the young boy's mind.

When the "Grito de Yara" echoed across Cuba, October 10, 1868, signalling the beginning of the Ten Years' War (the first Cuban war for independence from Spain), Martí was only fifteen, too young to join the *mambises*, as the revolutionary fighters for independence were called. But he did write a long epic poem "Abdala," glorifying the revolution and the fighters for independence, which was published in Mendive's journal, *La Patria Libre* (The Free Homeland). It was not long before Mendive was exiled, and Martí himself arrested and condemned to hard labor. The cause of his arrest was a letter he and his best friend, Fermín Valdés Domínguez, had written accusing a fellow student of being an apostate for having marched in a parade with the Spaniards. The authorities found the letter, and on October 21, 1869, the two boys were arrested and confined in the Havana city jail. Four and a half months later, on March 4, 1870, the two were tried by a court-martial. Martí's friend was given six months; he himself, insisting throughout the trial that he alone was responsible for the letter, received the harsh sentence of six years at hard labor in the government quarries.

Though still a boy, Martí spent six months in backbreaking stonecutting, which left him a physical wreck, half blind and with a hernia caused by a blow from a chain which troubled him the rest of his life. Thanks to army friends of his father, Martí spent only six months in the quarry, and was then transferred temporarily to a prison on the Isle of Pines. He was finally pardoned in January 1871, but to keep him from further seditious activities, the authorities deported him to Spain. Still half blind from the work in the sun and suffering from the hernia, he wrote to his great teacher, Mendive: "I have suffered much, but I am convinced that I have learned how to suffer. If I have had strength for it all and if I possess the qualities that make me a man, I owe it to you alone. From you I have acquired whatever Virtue and kindness there is in me."[1]

On January 15, 1871, Martí left for Spain, and from that day until April 11, 1895, when he landed with an expedition to head Cuba's Second War for Independence, he was to visit the island of his birth on only two brief occasions.

Martí completed his academic education at the universities of Madrid and Zaragoza. He read the classics, frequented literary salons, and went regularly to the theater. Yet while he continued his studies, he devoted much of his time in Spain to political agitation. Immediately after arriving in Madrid in January, 1871, he published a scathing denunciation of Spanish treatment of political prisoners in Cuba, *El Presidio Político en Cuba* (Political Prison in Cuba).[2] Written at the age of eighteen, it revealed Martí to be a writer of distinction and it had an important impact on liberal circles in Spain. "Pollice Verso" (Prison Recollections), published in Martí's collection of verses in 1882, contains additional comments on his prison experience. They are included below.

After he had arrived in 1871, Martí had looked forward to the day when Spain would become a Republic. Then, perhaps, Cuba might live harmoniously and peacefully with the mother country. But news came from Cuba that on November 27, 1871 a party of medical students at the University of Havana were seized by the pro-Spanish Volunteers, accused of having "profaned" the grave of Colonel Gonzalo Castañón, a reactionary editor who had been assassinated, presumably by Cuban rebels. Eight students were condemned to death, and shot at four o'clock the same morning. Some thirty others were sentenced to the chain gangs from four to six years.[3]

The news of the killing of the students wrought a complete change in Martí's outlook. The bloody incident destroyed forever all desire on his part for anything less than complete independence for Cuba, and he made a vow to devote his life to this cause.

Martí's sentence of confinement to Spain was finally lifted in January 1875. He had graduated from his university studies and passed examinations for the degree of Doctor of Philosophy and Humanities with outstanding grades. Since he had been exiled, he was unable to return to Cuba legally, especially during the period of war. In order to be closer to home and to join his parents, he settled in Mexico, after short stopovers in Paris and London. He spent almost two years in Mexico, earning his livelihood as a journalist, and achieving local prestige as a lecturer and orator. His play, *Amor con Amor se Paga* (Love is Repaid by Love), written for the Spanish actress Concha Padilla, was successfully presented in Mexico City, and he soon gained a reputation as a member of the literary salon of "Rosario de la Acuña," which spread throughout much of Latin America, and together with his writings, made him a figure of importance on the continent.

Martí participated in debates at the Hidalgo Lyceum, represented the workers at Chihuahua at a workers' congress, published articles in *Revista Universal*, dealing with art, drama and social issues, and in his newspaper articles and forum discussions devoted special attention to the plight of the Indian in Mexican society. ("Until the Indian is allowed to go forward, America will not begin to advance," Martí emphasized.) He also pleaded eloquently for the Cuban cause and raised funds for the revolutionary movement on the island.[4]

In January 1877, Martí returned to Cuba, landing in Havana under an assumed name—he used his second name, Julián, and his mother's maiden name, Peréz. He spent a month at home without being identified. But his precarious position made it virtually impossible for him to work, and he soon saw, too, that the cause of Cuban independence was lost for the time being. He therefore returned to Mexico and then went to Guatemala. There, thanks to a distinguished Cuban, José María Izaguirre, who had been appointed Director of the Normal School by liberal-minded President Justo Rufino Barrios, Martí found employment as professor of history and literature. In addition to teaching, he lectured, founded cultural clubs, helped edit the *Revista de la Universidad*, and wrote articles on the new civil code. Also while in Guatemala he wrote the play *Drama Indio*, and *La Niña de Guatemala*, one of his most famous poems.[5]

During this period Martí met Carmen Zayas Bazán, a beautiful daughter of a wealthy Cuban exile, whom he married on December 20,

1877. They lived in Mexico and Guatemala until the Ten Years War ended in 1878. A general amnesty was then declared by Spain, and the young couple was finally able to return and settle in Cuba.

When Martí and his young bride, expecting a child, returned to Cuba, they found things little better than before. The key provisions of the Pact of Zanjón ending the Ten Years' War, promising Cuba political concessions, proved to be a hoax. Disappointed and enraged, Martí spoke out against the Spanish duplicity and announced his willingness to support only those who would agree to work energetically for a radical solution to all of Cuba's problems. He made it clear that he believed that independence was the solution. Rights, he declared, were "to be taken, not requested; seized, not begged for."

Captain General Ramón Blanco, the Spanish governor, called Martí "a dangerous madman," and urged his immediate imprisonment. But under pressure from Martí's friends, he promised that he would not be brought to trial if he declared in the newspapers his adherence to Spain. "Tell the General that Martí is not the kind of man that can be bought," Martí replied. The result was deportation once again to Spain.[6]

On September 25, 1879, José Martí was deported under "surveillance" to Spain. During his brief stay in Cuba, he had become a father; his young bride had given birth to José Martí Zayas Bazán, to whom Martí was later to dedicate one of his loveliest collections of poetry, *Ismaelillo*. But by the time he left Cuba, his marriage was failing, for Carmen disapproved of his political involvements, and her husband was not one to allow domestic concerns to stand in the way of his revolutionary activities.

Escaping from his Spanish prison, Martí made his way to Paris, and then settled briefly in New York. Appointed a professor in Caracas, Martí left on March 21, 1881, for Venezuela, where he vowed to "arouse the world" to the Cuban cause. In addition to teaching he edited *Revista Venezolana*, the first issue of which came off the press on July 1, 1881. But his stay in Caracas was cut short by a dispute with the dictator-president, Guzman Blanco, and he left Venezuela on July 28 for New York.

Except for short trips to Mexico, Central America, Santo Domingo, and Jamaica, always in the interest of Cuban independence, Martí lived in the United States during the last fourteen years of his life. Most of these years were spent in New York or on visits to other cities, especially those like Tampa and Key West, Florida, in which there was an important colony of Cuban exiles, and most of his time was devoted to organizing for the second and final war for the independence of Cuba.

In 1881, Martí was twenty-eight. He was slightly built and of medium height, with a high forehead and penetrating eyes, slender and frail. His hands were artistically long and narrow, delicately shaped and always moving. He habitually dressed in black suits and a black silk bow tie. His clothes were never new because he led a very meager existence writing for his living in New York, but they were scrupulously cleaned and neatly pressed. Martí was constantly on the go and seemed to possess boundless energy. He wrote for leading newspapers in Latin America and for the New York *Sun*; he translated books into Spanish; he edited *Patria*, the organ of the Cuban Revolutionary Party, the party organized by Martí on January 5, 1892, after two years of intensive preparations, to lead the second war for independence. He published *La Edad de Oro* (The Golden Age), a magazine for youngsters; he wrote poetry, essays, articles, plays, and children's stories; he served as consul for Uruguay and Argentina. And all the time he spoke at countless meetings, many sponsored by Cuban tobacco workers in Florida and New York, and poured out a stream of pamphlets, articles, and essays for the Cuban revolutionary cause.[7]

On February 24, 1895, the *grito* or "cry" was sounded at Baire, a village about 50 miles from Santiago de Cuba, heralding the beginning of the second war for Cuban independence, a liberation movement brilliantly organized by José Martí. On April 1, 1895, Martí (in the company of the military leaders of the rebellion) left Montecristi, Santo Domingo, bound for Cuba. On April 11, he made his landing on the beach at La Playita in Dos Rios, eastern Cuba.

On May 18, Martí wrote from Dos Rios to Manuel Mercado, his friend in Mexico. The letter opened: "I am now, every day, in danger of giving my life for my country."[8] The letter was never finished. On May 19, the Spaniards attacked. Though ordered by the military leaders to remain with the rear-guard, Martí rode forth to his first encounter with the Spaniards. As he rode through a pass, Spanish soldiers in ambush shot him down. Attempts to retake Martí's body were futile. The Spaniards carried it away to Santiago de Cuba, where on May 27, 1895, José Martí was buried.

"He died," wrote Charles A. Dana of the New York *Sun*, a friend and admirer of Martí, "as such a man might wish to die, battling for liberty and democracy."[9]

José Martí was a rare combination of man of ideas and man of action. "Ideas were for him weapons in the fight for a better world, in which freedom for Cuba was the first step," one student has correctly observed. He was a man of many talents: a lawyer, a poet, a master of the Spanish language, a great orator, in many universities in Latin America a teacher of language, literature and philosophy, a distinguished journalist, a diplomat, and the organizer of every detail of the Cuban revolution. His writings made him so admired and respected throughout Spanish-speaking America that Argentina, Uruguay, and Paraguay made him their consular representative in the United States.

Martí's writings, collected and edited by Gonzalo de Quesada y Miranda, fill 70 volumes. Even this edition is incomplete since there still remains uncollected material scattered in South American newspapers.[10]

José Martí's prose writings occupy the great bulk of these volumes. Martí is that unusual kind of writer of whose prose and poetry we can think equally highly. The strength and rhythmical felicity of the prose are reflected in so much of the poetry—and vice versa. But probably more has been written of Martí the poet than of Martí the prose writer.[11] His poetry has earned him the enthusiastic praise of such distinguished authorities as Gabriela Mistral, Rubén Darío, Miguel de Unamuno, Fernando de los Ríos, Rufino Blanco, Fombona Amado Nervee, Ivan A. Schulman, Andrés Iduarte, Félix Lizaso, Juan Marinello, Federico de Onís, Ángel I. Augier, Guillermo Díaz Plaja, Eugenio Flout, Juan Carlos Giano, Emir Rodríguez Monigal, Alfredo A. Roggiano, Miguel de Cinamino y Jugo, Cinto Vitier, Manuel Pedro González, Juan Carlos Giano, and Roberto Fernández Retamar.[12]

Although the birth of Modernism as a movement is generally considered to have occurred with the 1888 publication in Chile of *Azul* (Blue), a collection of verse and prose by the Nicaraguan poet Rubén Darío, these and other critics point out that Martí's poetry opened the way for *modernismo* in Spanish American literature, and that Martí anticipated its key features—daring use of new rhythms and meters, broadening the resources of language in free verse, wide use of symbolism, and rejection of traditional principles of Spanish versification and excessive sentimentalism of Romanticism.

In his literary testament presented to Gonzalo de Quesada on the eve of his death, Martí criticized and classified his poetry within two short sentences: "None of my verses should be published before *Ismaelillo*. None of them are worth bothering with. Those which come afterwards to the end, are worth something. They are sincere."[13] Actually, Martí's verses prior to 1882, when *Ismaelillo* was published, reveal his great creative power. But they are very much influenced by the classical Spanish writers and are in the traditional vein. In his introductions to his greatest works of poetry, which "come afterwards", we can observe the difference in approach. In the preface to *Ismaelillo*, Martí writes:

> If someone tells you that these pages are like other pages, tell them that
> I love you too much to thus dishonor you.

In the introduction to *Versos Libres,* he writes:

These are my poems. They are what they are. I have not borrowed them from anyone. As long as I was unable to lock up my visions whole, and in a form worthy of them, I let them fly. Oh, how many old friends that have never flown! But poetry has its honesty. And I have always wanted to be honest. I know how to pare my poems, but I do not wish to do so. Just as every man has his own physiognomy, every inspiration has its own language. I love the difficult sonorities, the sculptural line: vibrant as porcelain, swift as a bird, scalding and flowing as a tongue of lava. . . .

I have never concocted poems for this one or that one, but trapped them from my very self. They are not written with academic ink, but with my own blood. . . . I love honesty and difficult sonorities even if they seem brutal.

Then in the introduction to *Versos Sencillos,* Martí writes:

These poems are printed because they have already been made public by the affection with which some good souls received them one night of poetry and friendship. And because I love simplicity and believe in the need of putting one's feelings into plain and honest forms.

Each one of these great poetic compositions is a reflection of the poet himself. Martí does not belong to those "exterior" poets who write verses to rhyme words. (And Martí dominated rhyme like a classicist.) But he belongs rather to those who write because of intimate necessity, to those who seek in verse the alleviation of their profound restlessness.

In April 1882 Thompson and Moreau of New York City published the short book of fifteen tender poems (with a brief prose introduction) by Martí about his son Pepe to whom he gave the name of Ismaelillo. At the outset there is a dedication which explains the reasons for the verses: "Fearful of everything I seek refuge in you." But there is also Martí's constant optimism, in the midst of disappointment and failures, in the victory of his cause. His son symbolized for Martí the Cuba of tomorrow, a free and independent homeland.

Ismaelillo was written in Venezuela the year before its publication while Martí's only son was living in Cuba. The heartbreak he experienced as a result of the separation is fully revealed in the fifteen poems. On the surface the verses seem motivated by a loving sense of humor on the part of a father toward his son. However, the depth of thought that is revealed upon closer examination, shows an intense feeling and almost passionate desire to be reunited with his son, for that reunion would also signify the liberation of his country and the end of Martí's exile from his beloved Cuba. In the spirit of teacher and reformer, the father included bits of the moral code and criticism of the existing situation, as he poured forth his lament as an explanation of the separation.

Martí dedicated his verses to the memory of the dwarf-like prince who is his son, and the poetry is a gay celebration that expresses the happiness of the father as he remembers the child and his pranks. He describes his dwarf-like prince, the child Pepe who has blond locks of hair, white locks, locks that denote his innocence. The boy's eyes are like those of his father; they fly with enthusiasm; they shine like the stars; they palpitate like the wind; they burn with desire and passion. The memory of the child's kisses, his smile, his games, are a constant source of joy to the father. The will of the dwarf-like prince is the father's command. Rubén Darío has observed that *Ismaelillo* is a book of poetry on the art of being a father.[14]

Martí explains that he is the vassal of his king of hearts, his son, just as men are the vassals and slaves of greater powers, and he has subjugated himself to the whim and fancies of his child prince. The poet pledges loyalty to Pepe, the symbol of a future and independent native land. At times, he experiences the torment of the separation and exile, but when the boy appears again in the dreams of the celebration he receives good counsel and explanations as to why this father must live in foreign lands against his will.

In the development of the poems, the positions of the father and son are reversed. The vassal of thought is Pepe, and he is to listen to and heed all the advice dedicated to him within the verses of *Ismaelillo*. He must realize that there is absolute truth in the statement that morality is important in life. If Pepe is to come under the domination of the devilish spirit and to desire a life of immorality and impurity, the father would prefer to see him dead rather than subjugated to the tyranny of the yellow king— who is the diabolic force—yellow denoting the stains of immorality, impurity, hate and deceit.

> But if you seem to love
> The yellow king
> Of the men,
> Die with me!
> To live impure?
> Don't live, my son![15]

In *Ismaelillo*, Martí departed from the style of verses he had written as a youth. These fifteen poems, as Rubén Darío and Juan Marinello have both emphasized, represent Martí the poet in the full maturity of his career of letters, and the work is truly a major element in Cuba's contribution to Latin American literature. With publication of *Ismaelillo*, Martí emerged as a first rate poet. Because of the simplicity of the verses, the book has been commonly recognized as one of the first utterances of the Modernist movement. In his study, *Precursores del Modernismo*, Torres Rioseco points to the departure in *Ismaelillo* from the antiquated romantic style,[16] while Eugenio Florit notes that this small book signifies the advent of a new literary school and the departure of Romanticism: "From this book, from this date, begins American Modernism." Finally, the distinguished Dominican critic Pedro Enrique R. Ureña writes: "Martí had no intention of starting a literary revolution, involved as he was in his plan of political insurrection. But 1882, the year in which *Ismaelillo* was published, should be considered as the starting date of a new tendency in our poetry, later known under the colorless title of Modernism."[17]

The poems in Martí's *Versos Libres*, written between 1878 and 1882, are another remarkable contribution to Hispanic American literature.[18] The verses are free in every sense of the word, free in form, unshackled, the subject matter being whatever troubled the sensitive soul of the poet at the moment. They were another stepping-stone on the way to Modernism.

The poems are the expression of Martí's love for freedom. The title itself reflects this sentiment. Rubén Darío, the father of Modernism, noted the play on the word "free."[19] They are free verses because they are written in a style that adheres to no special constant rhyme though the meter is the hendecasyllable (a verse of 11 syllables). The verses were written in Martí's own blood as he notes in the dedication: "Wounds are these of my own soul—my warriors. None has emerged overheated, artificial, recomposed, from my mind, but as tears stream from the eyes, and as blood spurts from a wound.[20]

The poet is the tortured lover of his native land, and though his body remained forever in exile, his heart was true to Cuba. The tormented man looks out upon the beautiful tropical fields, and observes that Cuba is in a state of slavery. His lips tremble with anger. He calls to mind the negligent and melancholic earth that is situated in the shadows of the overpowering bondage of impurity and immorality. His failure to attain his goal does not impair the strength of his iron will for the ideal of liberty. He exclaims that a basket of flames is to give hope to his generation of Cubans. He reveals the depth of his emotions:

Oh soul, good soul! Yours is a difficult task!
Kneel down, be still, submit, and lick
The sovereign's hands; exalt, forgive shortcomings,

Or have them—which is the best way
To forgive them—and, timorous and meek,
Rejoice in wickedness, enshrine the vanities,
And then you'll see, my soul,
Your poor man's empty dish transformed
Into a plate of richest gold!
But be on guard, oh soul,
For men today use tarnished gold!
So pay no heed—the fops and scoundrels
Make their trinkets out of gold,
But not their guns; their guns are made of iron![21]

The poet's life is symbolized in the comparison between the yoke that represents his bondage in life and the star that is the freedom from tormenting realities and the vices of society. The poet was born to be the hero of his native land, but meanwhile he suffers the torments of exile. He is no longer Cuban, but a stranger, a wandering traveler, without a specific country, who continues his journey from land to land in the Americas. He wishes to return home, but is compelled to complete his task. He prepares to die, for he has observed that a good soul can no longer exist on earth. He believes that the end of life brings the hidden salvation of humanity. He desires the kiss of death. He laments the never ceasing struggle of the patriots, and he condemns the traitors. He recalls how from early youth he fought for his ideal, for he loved life. And now, the poet longs for the flowers of heaven. In the meantime, he wishes to abandon himself to the wide open spaces.[22]

Eugenio Florit notes that Martí is never the artificial stylist, and that the Cuban poet, in the manner of the Romantics, does not scorn the use of the classical elements. But Martí, he emphasizes, gives them a greater freedom than previously. Juan Marinello observes that the grandiose theme and resulting episodes of the fight for freedom produce a poetry that approaches the traditional ode. Marinello adds that the free verses are a product of Martí's maturity, his sincerest ideas and ideals. Rubén Darío wrote that the "rough Hendecasyllabic (eleven-syllable) verses were born of great fears, of great hopes, or the insatiable love for liberty or of sad love." Miguel de Unamuno observed:

I read them twice and aloud; one of them I read to a blind friend of mine who is a poet. The obscurity, the confusion, even the disorder of these free verses enchanted us. This dishevelled, touselled poetry, unadorned, brought us the free wind of the forest, blocking off the vapors carrying those effeminate perfumes of the salon or those singable verses issuing from the swaying of the hammock, or the oversweet sing-song with which young ladies, who bang on the piano, amuse themselves.[23]

In June 1891 appeared the final complete book of poetry that José Martí was to publish during his lifetime.[24] Published by Louis Weiss and Company of New York City, the book carried the simple, unaffected title *Versos Sencillos*. It was dedicated to two friends, Manuel Mercado of Mexico and Henry Estrájulas of Uruguay. To Martí there is nothing so sacred as friendship, and though there may be treasures and material riches, for the poet the greatest jewels are his friends.

The poems were written during the summer of the previous year in the heart of the Catskill Mountains, where Martí had gone for a much needed rest to recover his health. As is almost all of his poetry, these verses are a self-portrait in which Martí opens his heart, mind and soul to view. Frankness and simplicity pervade every line. The first stanza of the first book is typical of the work:

> I am an honest man
> From where the palm trees grow;
> Before I die I want my soul
> To pour forth its poetry.[25]

In these simple verses, product of the mature Martí, there are elements of Romanticism, such as in the episodes of the mother who is in search of her son as he is in danger, the father who casts a blow at the traitor, who is his son, the dance of the Spanish ballerina, and the death and burial of the "niña de Guatemala." The poet remembers his parents. He calls to mind an incident during an uprising in his native city when his mother came to take him home. He recalls the deep respect the revolutionists displayed in the presence of his mother, with the removal of their hats, symbol of the struggle that had taken the life of a son. The good woman kissed her son, and prayed fervently in gratitutde to God for having kept the youthful fighter alive. The poet's thoughts wander to his father, the symbol of the homeland and its honor. The father who was a poor artillery man, a soldier, and a worker, is dead:

> I thought of the poor artillery man.
> He is in the tomb; quiet:
> I thought of my father, the soldier:
> I thought of my father, the worker.[26]

The description of the Andalusian ballerina is colorful and fiery, and the poet is intrigued by the body and physical aspects. The spectator is enveloped by the flame of the dancer's eyes and the fiery colored cloak. Forehead raised, cloak across the shoulders, arms lifted in an arc, she clicks her heels with the aid of the castanets, as though it were the rapid beating of hearts. The body sways and swerves and the mouth that is like a rose is opened, for the dancer is very tired. She returns to her corner with tremulous heart and all alone.[27]

In Guatemala his chess-playing took Martí into one of the best homes, that of the ex-President of the Republic, Don Miguel García Grandados, the father of five daughters: Adela, María, Christina, Leonor, and Luz. María suffered silently in her love for Martí, and when the poet married Carmen Zayas Bazán, she became despondent over the fact that her love had not been returned. When Martí brought back his bride from Mexico, her condition grew worse. When María died, Martí knew that she had died of love, and not of disease, as was reported. She is "la niña de Guatemala" in one of the most famous love poems in Latin American literature.

The poet recalls that María gave him a perfumed pin cushion when he was taking leave of her to go to Mexico. She presented that cushion to him so that he would not forget her, but he returned to marry another woman. The youth remembered the burial, and the kiss he had placed on her forehead for the last time.

The poet has little contempt for himself. Nevertheless, the thought and memory of María García Grandados are so beautifully told in the spirit of undying love that one cannot escape the conclusion that José Martí did love this young girl, perhaps as he loved his friends. Upon recalling the last kisses he gave to the young Guatemalan girl, Martí noted that hers was the forehead he had loved most in his life.[28]

The poet casts off the spell and returns to his fundamental theme of freedom and independence for Cuba, his native land. Martí was only a child when he saw for the first time the exploitation and abuse of the slaves. It was a beginning of his fight for freedom and equality:

A child saw him: He trembled
With passion for those who whimper:
And at the foot of death, he swore
To wash the crime with his blood!
I know of one great sorrow
Among the nameless ones:
The world's enormous sorrow
Is human slavery!

The child who witnessed the harsh treatment of the Negro slaves took it upon himself to side with the unfortunate ones:

> With the poor of the earth
> I wish to share my fate
> The mountain stream delights me
> More than the sea.[29]

José Martí was the poet and author of his death. It was his dream to die as a hero, for all good men die young and heroically. He would prefer, upon dying, a branch of flowers, which signified his love for Mother Nature, and a flag, which symbolized his desire for a free native land. José Martí was a sincere man from the land where the palm trees grow, and before his death, he wished to let the verses in his heart overflow.

In *Sound Patterns in a Poem of José Martí: Phonemic Structures and Poetic Musicality*, Ned Davison has made an admirable study of Martí's *Versos Sencillos*, the eighteen stanzas beginning "Yo soy un hombre sincero. . ." ("I am a sincere man"). He chooses these stanzas to analyze because, although they are well known, they are not normally identified as being "musical." Davison does not call Martí a musical poet. Nevertheless, he painstakingly notes the interplays of sound contained in the poem. He notes a "sense of order, suggesting discipline, control, and sureness," that provides credible structure for the poem.[30] Martí's insistent use of yo, for example, forms a phonemic and conceptual pattern. Davison devotes the latter half of his book to stanzaic plates, an unusual yet handy visualization of the sound patterns. This system of graphics adequately illustrates his phonemic analysis based on the poem's sounds.

With the publication of *Versos Sencillos*, Martí revealed that he was a master poet. The simple verses are the product of a deep thinker and master craftsman. It is hardly surprising that the vast bibliography of works dealing with Martí includes many articles, essays, and commentaries dealing with *Versos Sencillos*. Critic after critic has hailed the values and importance of the verses, and all agree that they are the most sincere expression of José Martí, poet.

When José Martí was about to leave for Cuba in 1895, he closed his career as a poet with a farewell poem:

> Adios. El vapor irá
> En la semana que viene:
> Ya lo tiene, ya lo tiene
> Un amigo que se va.

Yo de mi le he de decir
Que en seguirlo, sereno,
Sin miedo al rayo ni al trueno
Elaboro el porvenir

    Su
    José Martí[31]

Goodby. The boat leaves
Next week.
Now you have a friend
Who's leaving.

And of me I must say
That following serenely,
Without fear of the lightning and thunder
I am working out the future

    Your
    José Martí

José Martí the poet appeared at a moment of transition within Latin American culture and Spanish heritage. He rejected the foreign elements that were not in accord with the spirit of his native land, and with the use of enriched language, metaphors and similes, symbolic tones and colors, ushered in the literary movement that is purely Hispanic American and belongs exclusively to Latin America. In the process he announced the advent of Hispanic American Modernism. With *Ismaelillo* the embryo of the Modernist movement on the American continent was born.

Martí joins together the elements of the most elevated romanticism with symbolism, mysticism, the baroque tendencies, French influences, Spanish heritage, and Hispanic American culture. He announces the new and completely American literary movement with a wealth of language and with a great use of symbolism. All of Martí's poetry is rich in symbolism. Already in *Ismaelillo* there are numerous colors that signify certain qualities. The whiteness of innocence is joined with the white locks of Pepe, and the color of blood is the flame of the hero's soul. At times, the sadness of the poet is expressed with symbolic colors of vagueness, uncertainty, and mystery. But the poet's optimism triumphs, and the clouds are suddenly rosy with the poet's renewed strength. When the son appears again, the father's body is like a kissed rose, and he experiences a moment of joy. Rubén Darío has observed that rose color was the fundamental expression of Martí. "I believe," Darío wrote, "that just as Banville used the word 'lira' and Leconte de Lisle the word 'negro,' Martí most often used the word 'rose.' "[32]

The rainbow of red, green, yellow, rose, violet, black, and white tinctures of *Ismaelillo* continues to be present in the other verses of Martí, principally in the *Versos Sencillos*. Indeed, the *Versos Sencillos* are viewed as representing the mature stage and the highest point of Martí's development as a poet. In the prologue, the author clarifies his style: "I love the simpleness and believe in the necessity to put the sentiment in simple and sincere forms." But the simplicity of José Martí can be deceptive. Rubén Darío noted this difficulty in commenting on *Versos Sencillos*: "The simpleness of Martí is one of the most difficult to understand, because you don't get into it without a vigorous domination of the word and without much understanding.[33]

The verses are simple because the poet is of the people, and he cast his lot with the people, and therefore he has elevated the chromatic expressions of daily life to the art of verse. He would rather cast his lot with the impoverished ones on earth, for the brook pleases him more than does the vast sea. Here we have a clear illustration of a union based on the simplicity of form and complexity of thought. In *Versos Sencillos*, Martí takes the Spanish popular meter, the octosyllabic line, and converts the popular element of the Spanish classicists into a form that is dedicated to all of Hispanic America. Andrés Iduarte noted this popular element, and wrote: "Martí follows the *romance*, now you see, but he modifies and varies the *romance*. It is the best tradition always mixed with his natural originality. Those are the common classical verses, but not like all restored and renewed. It is the return to the classic, but with modern development."[34]

"Poetry must have its roots in the soil," Martí wrote, "and its base on real fact." He was the poet of the people because he understood the suffering of the poor. For he, too, had suffered. "My verses leap from pain," he wrote in the earlier *Flowers of Exile*, "as swords from their case when spurred by wrath, as the black waves with turbulent and high crests that whip against the tired sides of a ship in times of storm. It would be strange if the black shroud would open and a twig of roses should fall out."[35] In a letter to his friend Gabriel Zéndegui, written in July 1882, he discussed the poetry which had inspired his revolutionary duty, and that which was born of the most personal emotion. He says of *Ismaelillo*: "Not this time when I slept on a pillar of roses, could my head forget the pillow of stone on which I usually sleep; and the verses I make . . . are verses made from sleeping on a pillow of stone."[36]

Observing that the *Versos Sencillos* are born of the people, Gabriela

Mistral adds that "because of his popularist behavior, the verses of Martí reverberate in the ears and are fixed in the memory like a ringing tune."[37] "Martí," emphasizes Manuel Pedro González, "is the theoretician of authentic modernism. His poetry, so innovative and revolutionary, becomes like the theoretical base of the movement."[38] Martí takes the old elements of literary art—classical, mystical, conceptual, and romantic tendencies which are part of the Spanish tradition—and flavors them with the Hispanic temperament—brevity of poetry, stylistic color schemes, and symbolism with metaphors and images. His style changed as he matured. The earlier poetry was styled to suit the dramatic and fiery spirit of the youthful Martí, but more and more, the verses approach the final stages with their simplicity in form and complexity in thought and sentiment. However, the romanticist is still present in maturity, and he both goes backward to Spanish classicism and goes forward to Hispanic America. As Juan Marinello points out in writing of *Ismaelillo*: "While using the *seguidilla* (the Spanish stanza of four or seven verses), Martí had succeeded in both confirming and broadening 'the popular.' "[39]

In the poetic work of José Martí, hidden European influences and a Spanish literary basis may be found. But in reality the verses announce the birth of a new era in Latin American poetry. The verses of Martí are transitional, and with each poem, he moves toward a simplicity of form and depth of thought and sentiment that characterize his most mature poetic efforts. In his wish to express his sincerity and honesty with a wealth of language and individualism, he provides both the artistic purpose and tinctures of pure Modernism. Therefore, Rubén Darío, the father of the movement, called Martí "hijo" (son).[40]

But Federico de Onís shrewdly observes that Martí's modern tendencies reach points far beyond those of the Modernists. "His modernity points further than that of the Modernists, and today it is more valid and clear than it was even then."[41]

With his social preoccupations and spirit of reform, Martí reaches beyond stylistic endeavors emphasized by the Modernist school, reaches beyond the realm of pure poetic art, and includes the spirit of universality and philosophy within the lyric quality of his verses. "In Martí," wrote José A. Portuondo, "the often intimate and autobiographical verse does not shirk the collective problems. His own anxieties, along with everyone else's, are joined in the sorrowful or wrathful song that never falls into the commercial, for the poet expressed passionately what he truly feels, and the verse is not a poster, it is a confidant, it is the friend that comes to converse after the strenuous tasks of the day."[42]

As for Martí, himself, he summed it all up in his essay on Walt Whitman where he wrote:

Who is the ignoramus who maintains that people can dispense with poetry? Some persons are so short-sighted that they see nothing in fruit but the rind. Whether it unites or divides the soul, strengthens or causes it anguish, props it up or casts it down, whether or not it inspires a man with faith and hope, poetry is more necessary to a people than industry itself, for while industry gives men the means of subsistence, poetry gives them the desire and courage for living.[43]

NOTES

1. Philip S. Foner, *History of Cuba and Its Relations with the United States* vol.II(New York,1963), pp. 41, 65, 125, 134, 141, 162 173; Jorge Mañach, *Martí, Apostle of Freedom*, trans. Coley Tayor, introduction by Gabriela Mistral (New York, 1959), p. 76.

2. An English translation of *El Presidio Político en Cuba* (Political Prison in Cuba) appears in *Our America: Writings on Latin America and the Struggle for Cuban Independence*, translated by Elinor Randall, edited with an introduction and notes, by Philip S. Foner (New York, 1977), pp. 151-89.

3. Foner, *History of Cuba*, vol. II, pp. 176-77.

4. Mañach, *Martí*, pp. 134-36.

5. Félix Lizaso, *José Martí: Martyr of Cuban Independence*, trans. Esther E. Shuler (Albuquerque, New Mexico, 1953), pp. 135-38.

6. Mañach, *Martí*, p. 162.

7. For a detailed discussion of Martí's work in organizing the Second War for Independence, *see* Foner, ed. *Our America, passim*.

8. José Martí, *Obras Completas* (La Habana, 1946), vol. I, pp. 271, 285-93. Of the various collected works of Martí, this, the "Lex" edition, is the most convenient. The most complete, however, at present is "Editorial Trópico," published in Havana between 1936 and 1949.

9. New York *Sun*, May 23, 1895; Foner, *History of Cuba*, vol. II, p. 357.

10. What will probably be the first complete edition of Martí's writings and the first scholarly edition is now being prepared in Cuba by the Centro de Estudios Martianos, under the direction of Roberto Fernández Retamar.

    The following are Martí's writings available in English: *The America of José Martí*, edited and translated by Juan de Onís; *Martí on the U.S.A.*, edited and translated by Luis A. Baralt, and the four volumes translated mainly by Elinor Randall and edited, with introductions and notes by Philip S. Foner: *Inside the Monster: Writings on the United States and American Imperialism; Our America: Writings on Latin America and the Struggle for Cuban Independence; On Education: Articles on Educational Theory and Pedagogy, and Writings for Children from The Age of Gold*, and *On Art and Literature: Critical Writings.*

11. Manuel Pedro González makes the point that "Martí was the most read and admired prose writer in the Hispanic world in those years (between 1880 and 1900), and it was through his marvellous prose that young writers and poets became familiar with his poetry." *José Martí en el octogésimo aniversario de la iniciación modernista*, (Caracas, 1962,) pp. 16-17.

12. *See* Manuel Pedro González, *José Martí en el octogésimo aniversario de la iniciación modernista*, (Caracas, 1962); Ivan A. Schulman y Manuel Pedro González, *Martí, Darío y el modernismo*, (Madrid, 1969); Ivan A. Schulman, *Símbolo y color en la obra de José Martí*, (Madrid, 1960); Andrés Iduarte, *Martí, escritor*, (La Habana, 1951); Félix Lizaso, *Martí, místico de deber*, (Buenos Aires, 1940); Angel I. Augier, "Martí poeta, su influencia innovadora en la poesía de América," *Vida y Pensamiento de Martí*, (La Habana, 1942), vol. II, pp. 265-333; Rubén Darío, "Martí poeta," *Antología crítica de José Martí*, (Mexico, 1960), pp. 267-95; and Rubén Darío, "José Martí," in *Poesías Completas*, prologo y notas de Luis Alberto Ruix, (Buenos Aires, 1964), pp. 293-301; Guillermo Díaz Plaja, "Lenguage, verso y poesía en José Martí," *Cuadernos Hispanomericanos*, vol. XXXIX, 1953, pp. 312-22; Eugenio Florit, "José Martí, vida y obra, Versos," *Revista Hispánica Moderna*, vol. XVIII, 1952, pp. 20-71; Juan Carlos Ghiano, "Martí poeta," *Poesía (de Martí)*, (Buenos Aires, 1952), pp. 7-52; José Olivio Jiménez, "Un ensayo de ordinación transcendente en los 'Versos Libres' de José Martí," *Revista Hispánica Moderna*, vol. XXIV, 1968, pp. 671-84; Juan Marinello, "Martí: Poesía," *Anuario Martiano*, vol. I, 1969, pp. 117-65; Juan Marinello, *José Martí: Los Poetas*, (Madrid, 1972); Gabriela Mistral, *La lengua de Martí*, (La Habana, 1943); Emir Rodríguez Monegal, "La poesía de Martí, el modernismo," *Archivo José Martí*, 1953, pp. 38-67; Emir Rodríguez Monegal, "Sobre los Versos Libres de José Martí," *Archivo José Martí*, 1974, pp. 7-9; Miguel de Unamuno y Jugo, "Artas de Poeta," *Obras Completas* (Madrid, 1958), vol. VIII, pp. 573-77; Alfredo A. Roggiano, "Poetica y estilo de José Martí," *Humanitas* (Argentina), vol. I, pp. 351-

78; Cinto Vitier, *Los Versos de Martí*, (La Habana, 1969); Juan Carlos Ghiano, ed., *Poesía*, (Buenos Aires, 1952); Eugenio Florit, *Versos*, (New York, 1962).

13. Raimundo Lida, *Páginas Selectas de Martí*, Buenos Aires, 1939, p. 282.

What is probably Martí's first poem is "A mi madre" dated 1868. Other early poems of Martí include a family album, a recollection of imprisonment and resulting exile, fond memories and references to friends. They include poems published in various periodicals in Cuba, Mexico and New York. In general they represent the period of Martí's poetry which was characterized by pomp and splendor and stood in sharp contrast to the mature stage of simplicity of form and depth of thought. (Amelia Hipschman, "José Martí as a Poet," unpublished M.A. thesis, Columbia University, 1949, p. 29.)

14. Rubén Darío, "José Martí, poeta," *Archivo José Martí*, vol. VII, p. 336.

15. *See below* p. 14.

16. Torres Rioseco *Precursores del Modernismo*, (Madred, 1925), p. 86.

17. Eugenio Florit, "Notas sobre la poesía en Martí," *Archivo José Martí*, vol. IV, p. 19, Pedro Enrique Ureña quoted in José Martí: *Versos Seveillos y Otras Poemas*, (Madrid, 1952), pp. 6-7.

18. Though edited and arranged by Martí for publication, they were not published until 1913.

There are several excellent studies of *Versos Libres* including those by Cinto Vitier in *Antología Crítica de José Martí*, (Mexico, 1960); by Ivan A. Schulman in *José Martí, Versos Libres*, (Barcelona, 1970), and by Juan Marinello in *José Martí: Los Poetas*, (Madrid, 1972).

19. Rubén Darío, "José Martí, poeta," p. 337 and quoted in Iduarte, *Martí Escritor*, p. 101.

20. *Obras Completas*, vol. XX, p. 136.

21. *Ibid.*, p. 137.

22. *Ibid.*, p. 138.

23. Florit, "Notas", p. 22; Juan Marinello, "José Martí, Artista," *Reportario Americano*, San José de Costa Rica, vol. XXVI, Año XIV, p. 294; Darío, "José Martí, Poeta," pp. 338-39: Miguel de Unamuno quoted in José Martí, *Versos Sencillos y Otros Poemas*, (Madrid, 1952), pp. 7-8.

24. As we have noted in the case of *Versos Libres*, several of Martí's poetical works were published after his death. *Flores del Destierro*

(Flowers of Exile), poems of the youthful Martí, were published for the first time in Cuba in 1933. The *Versos de Amor*, published for the first time in Cuba in 1930, also belong to the youthful period of Martí's life.

25. *Obras Completas*, vol. XX, p. 149.
26. *Ibid.*, p. 151.
27. *Ibid.*, p. 153.
28. *Ibid.*, p. 162.
29. *Ibid.*, p. 164.
30. Ned Davison, *Sound Patterns in a Poem of José Martí: Phonemic Structures and Poetic Musicality*, (Salt Lake City, 1975), p. 45.
31. *See*, for example, "Los Versos Sencillos de José Martí," *Archivo José Martí*, vol. V, pp. 43-53.
32. Darío, "José Martí, poeta," p. 327.
33. "Martí en Darío," *Archivo José Martí*, vol. VII, p. 380.
34. Iduarte, *Martí, Escritor*, p. 134.
35. Editorial Lex, vol. I, p. 802.
36. Juan Marinello, *José Martí: Los Poetas*, p. 57.
37. Gabriela Mistral, "El silenco de los sencillos en Martí," *Alat*, Puerto Rico, 1939, vol. X, p. 14.
38. González, "José Martí en el octogésimo . . . .," p. 15.

     González correctly stresses that Martí's prose must also be considered as initiating the modernist movement in Latin America, and notes: "What historians and critics did not realize throughout 40 years, was the very essential and capital importance that prose had in the modern renaissance produced between 1880 and 1900." (*ibid.*, p. 17.)

39. Marinello, *José Martí: Los Poetas*, p. 72.
40. Iduarte, *Martí Escritor*, p. 33.
41. In Raimundo Lida, *Páginas Selectas de Martí*, (Buenos Aires, 1952), p. VII.
42. Quoted in *Trajectory and Actuality of Martí*, (Center of Studies on Martí, La Habana), 1961, pp. 39-40.
43. *On Art and Literature: Critical Writings by José Martí*, translated by Elinor Randall, with an introduction and notes, by Philip S. Foner (New York, 1981), p. 126.

Chronology of José Martí

1853, January 28: José Martí y Pérez is born in Havana, Cuba.

1865, March 19: Begins to attend the Municipal School for boys.

1868, October 10: Beginning of Ten Years' War.

1869, January 23: Date of first issue of *La Patria Libre* (*The Free Home-land*), a newspaper in which Martí collaborates and in which his drama *Abdala* is published.
October 21: Accused of treason, he is arrested and confined in the Havana City Jail.

1870, March 4: A court martial sentences him to six years in prison.
April 4: Sent to prison.
October 13: Sentence commuted and transferred to the Isle of Pines.

1871, January 15: Deported to Spain, leaves for Cadiz on the mail ship *Guipúzcoa*
January: His *El Presidio en Cuba* (*Political Prison in Cuba*) is published by the Ramón Ramirez printing shop.
May 31: Enrolls at the Central University of Madrid.

1873, February: Publishes *La República Española ante la Revolución Cubana* (*The Spanish Republic Before the Cuban Revolution*).

1874, January: Fall of the Spanish Republic. Delivers speech at public meeting organized to raise funds for the widows and orphans of the fallen Republicans.
June 30: Receives the degree of Bachelor of Civil and Canon Law.
August 31: Enrolls in all the subjects of the Faculty of Philosophy and Humanities.
October 24: Passes graduating examinations for the degree of Doctor of Philosophy and Humanities with outstanding grades.
December: Leaves Spain for Paris.

1875, January: Sails from Southampton for Mexico.
February 8: Arrives in Vera Cruz.
March 7: Work published in *Revista Universal*, magazine in Mexico.

April 7: Participates in debate on materialism and spiritualism at Hidalgo Lyceum.

May 5: Assumes publication of the "Bulletin" of *Revista Universal*, dealing with national affairs.

November 30: Last of his "Bulletins" appears.

December 19: Play *Amor con amor se paga* (*Love is Returned with Love*) presented at the Teatro Principal in Mexico City.

Represents Chihuahua workers at a workers' congress.

1876, November 19: Last issue of *Revista Universal* appears.

November 23: Entrance of Porfirio Díaz in the capital of Mexico, marking defeat of Lerdo regime.

December: Collaborates in *El Federalista*.

December 29: Sails for Havana.

1877, January 6: Arrives in Havana, using his middle name and second family name: Julián Pérez.

February 24: Sails for Vera Cruz using the same name, and from Mexico leaves for Guatemala, stopping at Belize, capital of British Honduras, and at Livingstone.

May 29: Appointed professor of French, English, Italian, and German literature and History of Philosophy at the Central School of Guatemala.

July: Gains recognition for speech at literary meeting at the Central Normal School.

September 15: Writes drama *Morazán*, to commemorate Independence Day. Work appears to be lost.

December: Authorized to move to Mexico.

December 20: Marries Cuban Carmen Zayas Bazán.

1878, January: Returns to Guatemala after leaving manuscript of booklet, *Guatemala*, to be published in Mexico.

April 6: Resigns post at the Central School.

Booklet *Guatemala* published in Mexico.

May: End of Ten Years' War for Cuban Independence.

July 6: Leaves Guatemala for Honduras.

August: Sails for port of Trujillo.

September 3: Arrives in Havana with his wife.

September 16: Asks permission to practice law. Request denied. Teaches in private schools.

November 12: Son, José Martí Zayas Bazán, is born.

1879, January 12: Appointed Secretary of Literary Section of the Guanabacoa Lyceum.

April 21: Speaks at reception in honor of the journalist Adolfo Márquez Sterling, and voices opposition to Autonomist policy.

April 27: Delivers eulogy of the violinist Díaz Albertini at the Guanabacoa Lyceum.

August 26: Outbreak of Little War for Independence.

September 25: Accused of conspiracy and deported.

December: Leaves Spain for Paris.

1880, January 3: Arrives in New York.

January 24: Delivers lecture at Steck Hall, later published under the title, "Cuban Affairs," New York, 1880.

February 21: Publishes first article on art in *The Hour*, weekly magazine in New York, and writes article in English.

May 13: Writes Proclamation of New York Revolutionary Committee in connection with arrival in Cuba of General Calixto García to assume leadership of the Little War.

October: Capitulation of General Emilio Núñez, last leader to give up arms, ends Little War.

Writes for New York *Sun*.

1881, March 21: Appointed professor in Caracas.

July 1: First issue of *Revista Venezolana*, edited by Martí, appears.

July: Dispute with Dictator Guzman Blanco forces him to leave Venezuela.

July 28: Departs for New York.

August 20: Begins sending articles from New York to newspaper *La Opinión Nacional* of Caracas.

1882, April: Book of poems *Ismaelillo* published. Writes most of *Versos Libres (Free Verse)* which remains unpublished.

July 15: Sends first article to *La Nación* of Buenos Aires, published September 13.

1883, March: Begins to collaborate in *La América* of New York.

July: Delivers speech on occasion of Bolívar centennial at Delmonico Hall.

October: Edits *La América*.

1884, January: Appointed New York correspondent of *La Sociedad Amigos del Saber* of Caracas.

October 10: Delivers first speech commemorating Grito de Yara, October 10, 1868
October 20: Writes letter to Máximo Gómez excluding himself from revolutionary plans of Gómez and Antonio Maceo.

1885: Publishes novel *Amistad Funesta* under pseudonym, "Adelaida Ral" in *El Latino-Americano* of New York.

1886: Becomes correspondent of *La República*, of Honduras.

1887, April 16: Appointed Uruguayan Consul.
Mother visits New York.

1888, February: Works on translation of poem "Lala Rookh" by Thomas Moore.
Appointed corresponding member of Academy of Sciences and Arts of San Salvador.
October 12: Becomes representative in the United States and Canada of association of "La Prensa" of Buenos Aires.

1889, March 21: New York *Evening Post* publishes his letter "Vindication of Cuba," later printed in booklet, *Cuba and the United States*.
Invited to become correspondent of *El Partido Liberal de Mexico*.
April 18: Sends first article to *La Opinión Pública*, of Uruguay.
July: Appearance of first issue of *La Edad de Oro* (*The Golden Age*) monthly publication dedicated to the children of America.
November 2: Writes articles, published in *La Nación* (Buenos Aires), warning Latin America that Pan-American Congress represents a move by expansionist forces in the United States to dominate Latin America economically and politically.
November 20: Speaks at meeting in Hardman Hall, in honor of the poet José María Heredia.
December 19: Speaks at meeting of Spanish-American Literary Society of New York in honor of delegates to the International American Conference (Pan-American Congress).

1890, January 22: Inauguration of The League, a society for the promotion of education, in New York. Becomes a teacher of the League for Negro workers.
June 16: Appointed Argentine Consul in New York.
July 24: Appointed Paraguayan Consul in New York.
December 23: Appointed Uruguayan representative to International

Monetary Conference in Washington.

December: Appointed chairman of the Spanish-American Literary Society of New York.

1891, March 30: Report read in English and Spanish at the Monetary Conference in Washington.

April: Speaks at meeting at Spanish-American Literary Society in honor of Mexico.

May: Publishes article on Monetary Conference warning Latin America of United States designs.

June: Speaks at meeting organized by the Spanish-American Literary Society, in honor of the Central American Republics.

Publishes *Versos Sencillos*.

October 11: Resigns post as consul of Argentina and Uruguay.

October 30: Resigns post as chairman of the Spanish-American Literary Society.

November 25: Visits Tampa at the invitation of the "Ignacio Agramonte Club."

November 27: Speaks at "Convención Cubana de Tampa."

Founds the League for Education in Tampa, similar to The League in New York, and joins Patriotic Cuban League.

November 28: His "Resolutions taken by the Cuban Emigrés in Tampa," considered as the preamble to the bases of the Cuban Revolutionary Party, approved.

December 25: Visits Key West at invitation of group of Cuban workers.

1892, January 3: Speaks at meeting organized by the "San Carlos Club."

January 4: Attends meeting of club "Patria y Libertad" (Homeland and Freedom).

Tours tobacco factories of Key West and addresses Cuban tobacco workers.

January 5: Presides over meeting of club presidents where agreement is reached to organize Cuban Revolutionary Party.

Writes bases and statutes of Cuban Revolutionary Party.

January 8: Submits program of the Cuban Revolutionary Party to the Tampa Patriotic League. Program unanimously approved.

January 21: League of New York holds meeting protesting letter in which Collazo and Roa slander Martí.

February 17: Makes report at meeting in Hardman Hall on his tour of Tampa and Key West.

March 14: Appearance of first issue of *Patria*.

April 18: <u>Elected delegate of Cuban Revolutionary Party</u>.
July: Tours Florida to organize support for Cuban Revolutionary Party.
August 4: Gives instructions to Major Gerardo Castellanos, first commissioner of Cuban Revolutionary Party, who is leaving for Cuba.
September 4: Leaves for Santo Domingo.
September 11: Meets with Máximo Gómez at La Reforma, Santo Domingo. Invites him to join new revolutionary movement for independence of Cuba.
September 24-October 13: Visits Haiti and Jamaica.
October 23: Reports on his tour at meeting of The League in New York.
November: Visits Tampa and Key West. In Tampa life endangered by plot to poison him.
December: Speaks at meeting of Spanish-American Literary Society of New York, in honor of Venezuela.

1893, January 31: At meeting in Hardman Hall Cuban Revolutionary Party publicly rejects autonomist policy.
February 1: Invites Antonio Maceo to assume leading position in liberation movement.
February-March: Tours Florida for Cuban Revolutionary Party.
April 10: Re-elected delegate of Cuban Revolutionary Party.
April: Visits Philadelphia for Cuban Revolutionary Party.
May 24: Delivers speech at Hardman Hall, giving an account of events in Cuba, and introduces Rubén Darío to meeting.
May 24: Issues communiqué in name of Cuban Revolutionary Party on events in Cuba.
May 26: Leaves for Santo Domingo.
June 3: Meets again with Máximo Gómez.
June 7: Delivers lecture at School of Law of Costa Rica, at the invitation of the Association of Students.
July 8: Visits Panama, en route to New York.
September: Tours Florida again for Cuban Revolutionary Party.
October 28: Speaks at meeting of the Spanish-American Literary Society in New York in honor of Bolívar.
December: Visits Philadelphia, Tampa, and Key West for Cuban Revolutionary Party.
Publicly thanked by clubs in Key West for "zeal, activity and good judgment" with which he has discharged duties as delegate.

1894, January 2: Intervenes in conflict in Key West resulting from introduction of Spanish workers from Cuba to break strike of Cuban tobacco workers in "La Rosa Española" factory, and brings about return of Spanish workers to Cuba.

April 8: General Máximo Gómez arrives in New York for discussion with Martí.

April 10: Re-elected delegate of Cuban Revolutionary Party.

May 4: Accompanied by Francisco Gómez, son of Máximo Gómez,
leaves for tour of Philadelphia, Key West, Tampa, Jacksonville, and
other cities.

May 30: Visits New Orleans.

June: Travels to Costa Rica, Panama, and Jamaica.

July 22: Visits Mexico and is greeted by *El Universal*.

December 25: Organizes Fernandina plan calling for expeditionary
force to leave for Cuba from Fernandina, Florida, pick up Maceo in
Costa Rica, and begin the War for Independence.

1895, January 10-14: Fernandina plan betrayed and exposed. U.S.
authorities detain three vessels and confiscate weapons of war.

January 29: Order for uprising in Cuba signed in New York.

January 31: Leaves for Santo Domingo.

February 24: "Grito de Baire," outbreak of the Second War for
Independence.

March 24: Writes letter to Federico Henríquez y Carvajal from
Montecristi, Santo Domingo, considered his political will and testament.

March 25: Writes *Manifesto of Montecristi*. Signed by Martí and
General Máximo Gómez.

April 1: Writes letter to Gonzalo de Quesada from Montecristi,
Santo Domingo, considered his literary will and testament.

Leaves on schooner from Montecristi for Cuba.

April 2: Arrives at Inagua.

April 5: With assistance of Haitian consul obtains passage on German fruit ship, *Nordstrand*, for Cape Haitian.

April 9: Leaves Cape Haitian.

April 11: Arrives at Inagua at dawn.

Sets sail for Cuba at 2 p.m. At 8 p.m. ship stops three miles off coast
of Cuba. Boards little boat with five companions and at about 11
p.m. lands on Playitas.

April 16: Proclaimed Major General before the Liberating Army.
Marches through the mountains of Baracoa in search of Antonio
Maceo.

May 2: Writes letter to editor of *New York Herald* explaining aims and methods of the Cuban War for Independence.

May 6: Meets at La Mejorana with Generals Máximo Gómez and Antonio Maceo. They agree on the strategy of the War.

May 18: Standing between Generals Gómez and Maceo, speaks to thousands of Cuban patriots in the Maceo encampment near Jagua.

May 18: Writes last letter—unfinished—to Manuel Mercado.

May 19: Killed in action at Dos Rios, Oriente Province, Cuba.

MAJOR POEMS OF
JOSÉ MARTÍ

ISMAELILLO

Hijo:

Espantado de todo, me refugio en ti.

Tengo fé en el mejoramiento humano, en la vida futura, en
la utilidad de la virtud, y en ti.

Si alguien te dice que estas páginas se parecen a otras páginas, diles que te
amo demasiado para profanarte así. Tal como aquí te pinto, tal te han
visto mis ojos. Con esos arreos de gala te me has aparecido. Cuando he
cesado de verte en una forma, he cesado de pintarte. Esos riachuelos han
pasado por mi corazón.

¡Lleguen al tuyo!

My son:

Daunted by everything, I take refuge in you.

I have faith in human betterment, in a future life, in the usefulness of virtue, and in you.

If someone should tell you that these pages resemble others, tell him I love you too much to thus dishonor you. I depict you here just as my eyes have seen you. You have appeared to me in these gala trappings. When I stopped seeing you in this way, I stopped depicting you. These rivulets have coursed through my heart.

May they reach yours!

Sueño despierto

Yo sueño con los ojos
Abiertos, y de día
Y noche siempre sueño.
Y sobre las espumas
Del ancho mar revuelto,
Y por entre las crespas
Arenas del desierto,
Y del león pujante,
Monarca de mi pecho,
Montado alegremente
Sobre el sumiso cuello,—
¡Un niño que me llama
Flotando siempre veo!

I Dream Awake

I dream with open eyes
Both night and day;
I always dream.
And on the spindrift
Of the wide rough sea,
And on the rolling
Desert sands,
And joyously astride
The humble neck
Of a mighty lion,
Monarch of my heart,
I always see a floating child
Calling to me!

Hijo, en tu busca
Cruzo los mares:
Las olas buenas
A ti me traen:
Los aires frescos
Limpian mis carnes
De los gusanos
De las ciudades;
Pero voy triste
Porque en los mares
Por nadie puedo
Verter mi sangre.
¿Qué a mí las ondas
Mansas e iguales?
¿Qué a mí las nubes,
Joyas volantes?
¿Qué a mí los blandos
Juegos del aire?
Qué la iracunda
Voz de huracanes?
A estos—ila frente
Hecha a domarles!
¡A los lascivos
Besos fugaces
De las menudas
Brisas amables,—
Mis dos mejillas
Secas y exangües,
De un beso inmenso
Siempre voraces!
Y ¿a quién, el blanco
Pálido ángel
Que aquí en mi pecho
Las alas abre
Y a los cansados
Que de él se amparen
Y en el se nutran

Errant love

To find you, son,
I cross the seas.
The kindly waves
Take me to you;
Fresh breezes
Cleanse my flesh
Of city
Worms;
But I am sad,
Since on the seas
I cannot shed my blood
For anyone.
What good are uniform
And tranquil waves
To me? What good
Are clouds, those flying
Jewels, to me?
What good to me
The soft winds playing,
And the raging voice
Of hurricanes?
The mind is made
To tame those things,
To tame the lustful
Furtive kisses
Of pleasant
Little breezes—
My two anemic
Sunken cheeks
Are ever avid
For an enormous kiss!
Whom does the pale
White angel, spreading
Her wings here
In my breast—the one
In whom the weary
May find sustenance
And shelter—

Busca anhelante?
¿A quién envuelve
Con sus suaves
Alas nubosas
Mi amor errante?
¡Libres de esclavos
Cielos y mares,
Por nadie puedo
Verter mi sangre!

Y llora el blanco
Pálido ángel:
¡Celos del cielo
Llorar le hacen,
Que a todos cubre
Con sus celajes!
Las alas níveas
Cierra, y ampárase
De ellas el rostro
Inconsolable:—
Y en el confuso
Mundo fragante
Que en la profunda
Sombra se abre,
Donde en solemne
Silencio nacen
Flores eternas
Y colosales,
Y sobre el dorso
De aves gigantes
Despiertan besos
Inacabables,—
¡Risueño y vivo
Surge otro ángel!

Whom does she seek
So eagerly?
Whom does my errant love
Enfold with soft
And misty wings?
Since seas and skies
Are free of slaves,
I cannot shed my blood
For anyone!

The pale
White angel weeps:
She weeps
From jealousy
Of heaven
That covers everyone
With varicolored
Clouds!
She folds
Her snowy wings
And hides
From them
Her desolate face—
And in the fragrant
Confused world
Unfolding
In deep shadows
Where colossal and eternal
Flowers sprout
In solemn silence,
And on the backs
Of giant birds—
Awaken
Endless kisses.
Lively and smiling,
Another angel appears!

Sobre mi hombro

Ved: sentado lo llevo
Sobre mi hombro:
¡Oculto va, y visible
Para mí solo!
Él me ciñe las sienes
Con su redondo
Brazo, cuando a las fieras
Penas me postro:—
Cuando el cabello hirsuto
Yérguese y hosco,
Cual de interna tormenta
Símbolo torvo,
Como un beso que vuela
Siento en el tosco
Cráneo: ¡su mano amansa
El bridón loco!—
Cuando en medio del recio
Camino lóbrego,
Sonrío, y desmayado
Del raro gozo,
La mano tiendo en busca
De amigo apoyo,—
Es que un beso invisible
Me da el hermoso
Niño que va sentado
Sobre mi hombro.

Upon my shoulder

Look, I carry him
Upon my shoulder,
Hidden and visible
To me alone.
When I bow down
To cruel afflictions,
He circles my head
With his round arm.
When sullenly
My bristling hair
Stands straight,
Grim symbol
Of an inner storm,
I feel his gentle hand
On my rude skull
Like a rapid kiss.
His hand is soothing
To this maddened steed!
When, midway upon
A dark and arduous road
I reach out
For some fond support,
I smile, dismayed
By rare enjoyment—
The handsome child
Upon my shoulder
Gives me an unseen kiss.

¡Venid, tábanos fieros,
Venid, chacales,
Y muevan trompa y diente
Y en horda ataquen,
Y cual tigre a bisonte
Sitienme y salten!
¡Por aquí, verde envidia!
¡Tú, bella carne,
En los dos labios muérdeme:
Sécame: mánchame!
¡Por acá, los vendados
Celos voraces!
¡Y tú, moneda de oro,
Por todas partes!
¡De virtud mercaderes,
Mercadeadme!
Mató el Gozo a la Honra:
Venga a mí,— ¡y mate!

Cada cual con sus armas
Surja y batalle:
El placer, con su copa;
Con sus amables
Manos, en mirra untadas,
La virgen ágil;
Con su espada de plata,
El diablo bátame:—
¡La espada cegadora
No ha de cegarme!

Asorde la caterva
De batallantes:
Brillen cascos plumados
Como brillasen
Sobre montes de oro
Nieves radiantes:
Como gotas de lluvia

Savage gadflies

Come, you savage gadflies;
Come, you jackals,
Propel your fangs and teeth,
Attack me in hordes.
Leap and lay siege
As tigers charge bisons!
This way, green envy!
And you, fair flesh,
Bite my two lips,
Annoy and defile me!
This way, voracious
Blinded jealousy!
And you, gold coins,
Are everywhere!
Merchants of virtue,
Barter with me!
Joy has killed Honor;
Come to me, and kill!

Let all come forth
And fight with their arms:
Pleasure with its cup,
The nimble virgin
With her kindly hands
Anointed with myrrh.
Strike me, oh devil,
With your silver sword—
The blinding sword
Must not blind me!

Let legions deafen
With clashing arms;
Let plumed helmets shine
Like gleaming snows
On golden mountains;
Let throngs of swords
And flags

Las nubes lancen
Muchedumbre de aceros
Y de estandartes:
Parezca que la tierra,
Rota en el trance,
Cubrió su dorso verde
De áureos gigantes:
Lidiemos, no a la lumbre
Del sol suave,
Sino al funesto brillo
De los cortantes
Hierros: rojos relámpagos
La niebla tajen:
Sacudan sus raíces
Libres los árboles:
Sus faldas trueque el monte
En alas ágiles:
Clamor oígase, como
Si en un instante
Mismo, las almas todas
Volando ex cárceres,
Rodar a sus pies vieran
Su hopa de carnes:
Cíñame recia veste
De amenazantes
Astas agudas: hilos
Tenues de sangre
Por mi piel rueden leves
Cual rojos áspides:
Su diente en lodo afilen
Pardos chacales:
Lime el tábano terco
Su aspa volante:
Muérdame en los dos labios
La bella carne:—
¡Que ya vienen, ya vienen
Mis talismanes!
Como nubes vinieron
Esos gigantes:
¡Ligeros como nubes
Volando iránse!

Stab clouds
Like raindrops;
Let it appear that earth,
Destroyed in its last days,
Has covered its green back
With golden giants.
Let us wage war, not
In the gentle sunlight
But in the dismal brilliance
Of sharp swords; let the red lightning
Cleave the mists;
And trees,
Shake free your roots;
Mountains,
Convert your slopes
To agile wings;
Hear outcries as if
At one same instant
Every soul
Set free and flying
Had seen its fleshly garb
Drop to its feet.
Clothe me with the rude
Attire of sharp
And menacing lances;
Let slender
Threads of blood
Course down my skin
Like scarlet asps;
Brown jackals,
Sharpen your fangs on mud.
Tenacious gadflies,
Polish your flying wings;
Fair flesh,
Bite my two lips—
For now my talismans
Are coming, they now
Are coming!
Those giants came
Like clouds;
Nimble as clouds
They'll vanish!

La desdentada envidia
Irá, secas las fauces,
Hambrienta, por desiertos
Y calcinados valles,
Royéndose las mondas
Escuálidas falanges;
Vestido irá de oro
El diablo formidable,
En el cansado puño
Quebrada la tajante;
Vistiendo con sus lágrimas
Irá, y con voces grandes
De duelo, la Hermosura
Su inútil arreaje:—
Y yo en el agua fresca
De algún arroyo amable
Bañaré sonriendo
Mis hilillos de sangre.

Ya miro en polvareda
Radiosa evaporarse
Aquellas escamadas
Corazas centellantes:
Las alas de los cascos
Agítanse, debátense,
Y el casco de oro en fuga
Se pierde por los aires.
Tras misterioso viento
Sobre la hierba arrástranse,
Cual sierpes de colores,
Las flámulas ondeantes.
Junta la tierra súbito
Sus grietas colosales
Y echa su dorso verde
Por sobre los gigantes:
Corren como que vuelan
Tábanos y chacales,
Y queda el campo lleno
De un humillo fragante,
De la derrota ciega

Hungry toothless envy,
Its gullet parched,
Will go through deserts
And calcined valleys
Gnawing on unadulterated
Squalid phalanxes.
The formidable devil
Will be attired
In golden garments,
His shattered blade
Clutched in his weary fist;
With loud laments
Of sorrow,
Beauty will clothe
Her useless finery
With tears—
And I, in the cool waters
Of some pleasant stream,
Will smile and bathe
My trickling blood.

I watch those
Scaled and gleaming
Cuirasses evaporate
In radiant dust clouds.
The helmets' visors
Flutter and argue;
The fleeing golden helmets
Vanish in air.
Behind a mysterious wind
The waving pennants
Trail in the grass
Like colored snakes.
Suddenly the earth
Seals shut its giant crevices
And hurls its verdant back
Upon the giants;
Gadflies and jackals
Fly as they run,
And fields are filled
With fragrant mists.
Evoking silent captains,

Los gritos espantables
Escúchanse, que evocan
Callados capitanes;
Y mésase soberbia
El áspero crinaje,
Y como muere un buitre
Expira sobre el valle:
En tanto, yo a la orilla
De un fresco arroyo amable,
Restaño sonriendo
Mis hilillos de sangre.

¡No temo yo ni curo
De ejércitos pujantes,
Ni tentaciones sordas,
Ni vírgenes voraces!
Él vuela en torno mío,
Él gira, él para, él bate;
Aquí su escudo opone;
Allí su clava blande;
A diestra y a siniestra
Mandobla, quiebra, esparce;
Recibe en su escudillo
Lluvia de dardos hábiles;
Sacúdelos al suelo,
Bríndalo a nuevo ataque.
¡Ya vuelan, ya se vuelan
Tábanos y gigantes!—
Escúchase el chasquido
De hierros que se parten;
Al aire chispas fúlgidas
Suben en rubios haces;
Alfómbrase la tierra
De dagas y montantes;
¡Ya vuelan, ya se esconden
Tábanos y chacales!—

The frightful cries
Speak pompously, affectedly,
Of blind defeat,
And pride tears out
Its long coarse hair,
Expiring in the valley
The way a vulture dies.
Meanwhile, upon the banks
Of a cool and pleasant
Stream, I smile
And stanch my flow
Of trickling blood.

I neither fear
Nor minister
To powerful armies
Or mute temptations
Or ravenous virgins!
He hovers about me,
Pauses, turns, and strikes;
His shield repels
Aggression here,
He swings his war club there;
He crushes, scatters,
And deals two-handed blows
To right and left.
His little shield fends off
A rain of well-aimed arrows;
He shakes them to the ground,
Presents a new attack.
The gadflies and giants
Fly, they fly away!
The cracking sound
Of breaking swords
Is heard.
Bright sparks ascend
In golden clusters;
The ground is carpeted
With swords and daggers;
Gadflies and jackals
Fly away and hide!—

Él como abeja zumba,
Él rompe y mueve el aire,
Detiénese, ondea, deja
Rumor de alas de ave:
Ya mis cabellos roza;
Ya sobre mi hombro párase;
Ya a mi costado cruza;
Ya en mi regazo lánzase;
¡Ya la enemiga tropa
Huye, rota y cobarde!
¡Hijos, escudos fuertes
De los cansados padres!
¡Venga mi caballero,
Caballero del aire!
¡Véngase mi desnudo
Guerrero de alas de ave,
Y echemos por la via
Que va a ese arroyo amable,
Y con sus aguas frescas
Bañe mi hilo de sangre!
¡Caballeruelo mío!
¡Batallador volante!

He buzzes like a bee,
Breaks through the air
And stirs it;
He pauses, soars,
And leaves behind
The sound of a bird's wing;
He brushes against my hair,
Rests on my shoulder,
Passes beside me
And jumps into my lap.
The hostile troops
Escape in rout and cowardice!
Sons, strong shields
For weary fathers!
Come, my knight,
My knight of air!
Come, my naked warrior
With the wings of a bird,
Let us set out
Upon the road
To that pleasant stream,
And let its cooling waters
Bathe my trickling blood!
My little knight!
My flying warrior!

VERSOS
SENCILLOS

MIS amigos saben como se me salieron estos versos del corazón. Fue aquel invierno de angustia, en que por ignorancia, o por fé fanática, o por miedo, o por cortesía, se reunieron en Washington, bajo el águila temible, los pueblos hispanoamericanos. ¿Cuál de nosotros ha olvidado aquel escudo, el escudo en que el águila de Monterrey y de Chapultepec, el águila de López y de Walker, apretaba en sus garras los pabellones todos de la América? Y la agonía en que viví, hasta que pude confirmar la cautela y el brío de nuestros pueblos; y el horror y vergüenza en que me tuvo el temor legítimo de que pudiéramos los cubanos, con manos parricidas, ayudar el plan insensato de apartar a Cuba, para bien único de un nuevo amo disimulado, de la patria que la reclama y en ella se completa, de la patria hispanoamericana, —que quitaron las fuerzas mermadas por dolores injustos. Me echó el médico al monte: 'corrían arroyos, y se cerraban las nubes: escribí versos. A veces ruge el mar, y revienta la ola, en la noche negra, contra las rocas del castillo ensangrentado: a veces susurra la abeja, merodeando entre las flores.

¿Por qué se publica esta sencillez, escrita como jugando, y no mis encrespados *Versos libres*, mis endecasílabos hirsutos, nacidos de grandes miedos, or de grandes esperanzas, o de indómito amor de libertad, o de amor doloroso a la hermosura, como riachuelo de oro natural, que va entre arena y aguas turbias y raíces, o como hierro caldeado, que silba y chispea, o como surtidores candentes? ¿Y mis *Versos cubanos*, tan llenos de enojo, que están mejor donde no se les ve? ¿Y tanto pecado mío escondido, y tanta prueba ingenua y rebelde de literatura? ¿Ni a qué exhibir ahora, con ocasión de estas flores silvestres, un curso de mi poética, y decir por qué repito un consonante de propósito, o los gradúo y agrupo de modo que vayan por la vista y el oído al sentimiento, o salto por ellos, cuando no pide rimas ni soporta repujos la idea tumultuosa? Se imprimen estos versos porque el afecto con que los acogieron, en una noche de poesía y amistad, algunas almas buenas, los ha hecho ya públicos. Y porque amo la sencillez, y creo en la necesidad de poner el sentimiento en formas llanas y sinceras.

José Martí
Nueva York: 1891

Simple Poetry

MY friends know how these poems have come from my heart. It was that grievous winter when, out of ignorance or a fanatical faith or fear or courtesy, the Spanish American nations met in Washington under the dreaded eagle. Who of us has forgotten that coat of arms bearing the eagle of Monterrey and Chapultepec,[1] of Lopez[2] and Walker,[3] with all the flags of America clutched in its talons? And the agony in which I lived until I could confirm the wisdom and enterprise of our nations? And the shame and horror in whose grip I was held by the legitimate fear that we Cubans might with parricidal hands aid the senseless plan to separate Cuba, for the sole good of another crafty master, from the fatherland that claims her and perfects itself in her, from the Spanish American fatherland?—for the forces depleted by unjust afflictions were taken away.

So the doctor sent me off to the mountains. Streams were running there, and clouds were closing in; I wrote some poetry. At times the sea roars, and in the dark of night its waves break against the bloodstained fortress; at times the bees buzz softly and forage among the flowers.

Why do they publish this simplicity, written as if in play, and not my boisterous *Free Verse*, my hirsute hendecasyllables born of great fears or great hopes or the indomitable love of freedom or a painful love of beauty, like a rivulet of pure gold flowing among the sands and roots and turbid waters, or like molten iron hissing and throwing sparks, or like incandescent fountains? And my *Cuban Poetry*, so filled with anger that it is better left unseen? And all those hidden sins of mine, and all those ingenuous and rebellious samples of literature? And why at this time, on the pretext of these wildflowers, exhibit a collection of my poetics and tell why I purposely repeat a rhyming word, or why I classify and group those words so they reach one's sentiments through sight and hearing, or why I leap over them when the tumultuous idea demands no rhyme or bears no repoussé? These poems are printed because the affection with which some kind souls received them, on one night of poetry and friendship, have made them public. And because I love simplicity and believe in the need to put feelings into plain and sincere forms.

New York, 1891[4]

1

Yo soy un hombre sincero
De donde crece la palma,
Y antes de morirme quiero
Echar mis versos del alma.

Yo vengo de todas partes,
Y hacia todas partes voy:
Arte soy entre las artes,
En los montes, monte soy.

Yo sé los nombres extraños
De las yerbas y las flores,
Y de mortales engaños,
Y de sublimes dolores.

Yo he visto en la noche oscura
Llover sobre mi cabeza
Los rayos de lumbre pura
De la divina belleza.

Alas nacer vi en los hombros
De las mujeres hermosas:
Y salir de los escombros,
Volando las mariposas.

He visto vivir a un hombre
Con el puñal al costado,
Sin decir jamás el nombre
De aquella que lo ha matado

Rápida, como un reflejo,
Dos veces vi el alma, dos:
Cuando murió el pobre viejo,
Cuando ella me dijo adiós.

I

I am an honest man
From where the palms grow;
Before I die I want my soul
To shed its poetry.

I come from everywhere,
To everywhere I'm bound:
An art among the arts,
A mountain among mountains.

I know the unfamiliar names
Of grasses and of flowers,
Of fatal deceptions
And exalted sorrows.

On darkest nights I've seen
Rays of the purest splendor
Raining upon my head
From heavenly beauty.

I've seen wings sprout
From handsome women's shoulders,
Seen butterflies fly out
Of rubbish heaps.

I've seen a man who lives
With a dagger at his side,
Never uttering the name
Of his murderess.

Twice, quick as a wink, I've seen
The soul: once when a poor
Old man succumbed, once when
She said goodby.

Temblé una vez—en la reja,
A la entrada de la viña,—
Cuando la bárbara abeja
Picó en la frente a mi niña.

Gocé una vez, de tal suerte
Que gocé cual nunca:—cuando
La sentencia de mi muerte
Leyó el alcaide llorando.

Oigo un suspiro, a través
De las tierras y la mar,
Y no es un suspiro,—es
Que mi hijo va a despertar.

Si dicen que del joyero
Tome la joya mejor,
Tomo a un amigo sincero
Y pongo a un lado el amor.

Yo he visto al águila herida
Volar al azul sereno
Y morir en su guarida
La víbora del veneno.

Yo sé bien que cuando el mundo
Cede, lívido, al descanso,
Sobre el silencio profundo
Murmura el arroyo manso.

Yo he puesto la mano osada,
De horror y júbilo yerta,
Sobre la estrella apagada
Que cayó frente a mi puerta.

Oculto en mi pecho bravo
La pena que me lo hiere:
El hijo de un pueblo esclavo
Vive por él, calla y muere.

Once I shook with anger
At the vineyard's iron gate
When a savage bee attacked
My daughter's forehead.

Once I rejoiced as I
Had never done before,
When the warden, weeping, read
My sentence of death.

I hear a sigh across
The land and sea; it is
No sigh: it is my son
Waking from sleep.

If I am said to take
A jeweler's finest gem,
I take an honest friend,
Put love aside.

I've seen a wounded eagle
Fly to the tranquil blue,
And seen a snake die in its
Hole, of venom.

Well do I know that when
The livid world yields to repose,
The gentle brook will ripple on
In deepest silence.

I've laid a daring hand,
Rigid from joy and horror,
Upon the burnt-out star that fell
Before my door.

My manly heart conceals
The pain it suffers; sons of
A land enslaved live for it
Silently, and die.

Todo es hermoso y constante,
Todo es música y razón,
Y todo, como el diamante,
Antes que luz es carbón.

Yo sé que el necio se entierra
Con gran lujo y con gran llanto—
Y que no hay fruta en la tierra
Como la del camposanto.

Callo, y entiendo, y me quito
La pompa del rimador:
Cuelgo de un árbol marchito
Mi muceta de doctor.

All is permanence and beauty,
And all is melody and reason,
And all, like diamonds rather
Than light, is coal.

I know that fools are buried
Splendidly, with floods of tears,
And that no fruit on earth
Is like the graveyard's.

I understand, keep still,
Cast off the versifier's pomp,
And hang my doctoral robes upon
A withered tree.

Yo sé de Egipto y Nigricia,
Y de Persia y Xenophonte;
Y prefiero la caricia
Del aire fresco del monte.

Yo sé las historias viejas
Del hombre y de sus rencillas;
Y prefiero las abejas
Volando en las campanillas.

Yo sé del canto del viento
En las ramas vocingleras:
Nadie me diga que miento,
Que lo prefiero de veras.

Yo sé de un gamo aterrado
Que vuelve al redil, y expira,—
Y de un corazón cansado
Que muere oscuro y sin ira.

Que él tiene salvo vasto de cosas intelectuales
pero él prefiere lo natural, la que es bella
y sencilla

II

I know about Persia and Xenophon,
Egypt and the Sudan,
But I prefer to be caressed
By fresh mountain air.

I know the age-old history
Of human grudges,
But I prefer the bees that fly
Among the bellflowers.

I know the songs that breezes sing
In the chattering branches;
Don't tell me that I lie—
I do prefer them.

I know about the frightened buck
Returned to its pen, expiring;
I know that weary hearts die darkly
But free from anger.

III

Odio la máscara y vicio
Del corredor de mi hotel:
Me vuelvo al manso bullicio
De mi monte de laurel.

Con los pobres de la tierra
Quiero yo mi suerte echar:
El arroyo de la sierra
Me complace más que el mar.

Denle al vano el oro tierno
Que arde y brilla en el crisol:
A mí denme el bosque eterno
Cuando rompe en él el sol.

Yo he visto el oro hecho tierra
Barbullendo en la redoma:
Prefiero estar en la sierra
Cuando vuela una paloma.

Busca el obispo de España
Pilares para su altar;
¡En mi templo, en la montaña,
El álamo es el pilar!

Y la alfombra es puro helecho,
Y los muros abedul,
Y la luz viene del techo,
Del techo de cielo azul.

El obispo, por la noche,
Sale, despacio, a cantar:
Monta, callado, en su coche,
Que es la piña de un pinar.

III

Hating the subterfuge and vice
In the halls of my hotel,
I go back to the gentle rustlings
Of my laurel hill.

I want to cast my lot
With the humble of this world;
A mountain brook means more to me
Than does the sea.

Give to the vain the yielding gold
That melts and glistens in the crucible,
But give me the eternal woods
When the sun breaks through.

I've seen gold turn to dirt
When prattling in the crucible,
But I prefer to seek the hills
When a dove is flying.

The Spanish bishop searches for
Some columns for his altar,
But in my mountain sanctuary
The poplars are columns!

The carpet is of solid fern,
The walls are made of birches;
Light filters through from the roof—
The blue sky roof.

At night the bishop comes
At his slow pace, to sing;
And quietly mounts his coach,
His pinecone coach.

Las jacas de su carroza
Son dos pájaros azules:
Y canta el aire y retoza,
Y cantan los abedules.

Duermo en mi cama de roca
Mi sueño dulce y profundo:
Roza una abeja mi boca
Y crece en mi cuerpo el mundo.

Brillan las grandes molduras
Al fuego de la mañana,
Que tiñe las colgaduras
De rosa, violeta y grana.

El clarín, solo en el monte,
Canta al primer arrebol:
La gasa del horizonte
Prende, de un aliento, el sol.

Díganle al obispo ciego,
Al viejo obispo de Espana
Que venga, que venga luego,
A mi templo, a la montaña!

The ponies pulling his coach
Are two blue birds;
The breezes croon and frolic,
The birches sing.

I sleep on a bed of rocks,
A deep and gentle sleep;
A bee grazes my mouth,
My inner world expands.

The vast green carvings shine
In the fires of dawn that tint
The hanging foliage with violet,
Rose and scarlet.

One lone bugle upon the hill
Heralds the first red clouds;
Horizon's haze is seized by the sun
With a single breath.

Advise the blind bishop from Spain,
The elderly Spanish bishop,
To come to my church at once,
My church in the hills!

V

Si ves un monte de espumas,
Es mi verso lo que ves:
Mi verso es un monte, y es
Un abanico de plumas.

Mi verso es como un puñal
Que por el puño echa flor:
Mi verso es un surtidor
Que da un agua de coral.

Mi verso es de un verde claro
Y de un carmín encendido:
Mi verso es un ciervo herido
Que busca en el monte amparo.

Mi verso al valiente agrada:
Mi verso, breve y sincero,
Es del vigor del acero
Con que se funde la espada.

V

Should you see a hill of foam,
It is my poetry you see;
My poems are mountains
And feather fans.

My poems are daggers
Sprouting blossoms from the hilts;
My poems are fountains
Spraying jets of coral.

My poems are palest green
And flaming scarlet;
A wounded deer that searches for
A refuge in the forest.

My poems please the valiant;
Sincere and brief, my poetry
Is rugged as the steel they use
To forge a sword.

VIII

Yo tengo un amigo muerto
Que suele venirme a ver:
Mi amigo se sienta, y canta;
Canta en voz que ha de doler.

En un ave de dos alas
Bogo por el cielo azul: *lo natural*
Un ala del ave es negra,
Otra de oro Caribú.

El corazón es un loco
Que no sabe de un color:
O es su amor de dos colores,
O dice que no es amor.

Hay una loca más fiera
Que el corazón infeliz:
La que le chupó la sangre
Y se echó luego a reír.

Corazón que lleva rota
El ancla fiel del hogar,   *→ Home*
Va como barca perdida,   *la importancia*
Que no sabe a dónde va.

En cuanto llega a esta angustia
Rompe el muerto a maldecir:
Le amanso el cráneo: lo acuesto:
Acuesto el muerto a dormir.

VIII

I have a dead companion
Who often comes to see me;
My friend sits down and sings,
Sings in a doleful tone.

"I row through azure skies
On a two-winged bird;
The bird has one black wing,
And one of a caribou gold.

"The heart is a lunatic
Who knows no single color;
Its love is either double-hued,
Or says it isn't love.

"There is a wilder lunatic
Than a heart bereft of joy:
She who has sucked its blood,
Then burst out laughing.

"A heart whose loyal anchor
To home and hearth is sundered
Is like a ship at sea
That has lost its way."

Upon this bitter note
The corpse starts cursing.
I stroke its head, put it to bed,
And let it sleep.

IX

Quiero, a la sombra de una ala,
Contar este cuento en flor:
La niña de Guatemala,
La que se murió de amor.

Eran de lirios los ramos,
Y las orlas de reseda
Y de jazmín: la enterramos
En una caja de seda.

. . . Ella dio al desmemoriado
una almohadilla de olor:
Él volvió, volvió casado:
Ella se murió de amor.

Iban cargándola en andas
Obispos y embajadores:
Detrás iba el pueblo en tandas,
Todo cargado de flores.

. . . Ella, por volverlo a ver,
Salió a verlo al mirador:
Él volvió con su mujer:
Ella se murió de amor.

Como de bronce candente
Al beso de despedida
Era su frente ¡la frente
Que más he amado en mi vida!

. . . Se entró de tarde en el río,
La sacó muerta el doctor:
Dicen que murió de frío:
Yo sé que murió de amor.

In the shadow of a wing
I wish to tell this flowered tale
Of the girl from Guatemala
Who died of love.

The wreaths were of lilies
And jasmine and mignonette;
We laid the girl to rest
In a silken casket.

. . . She gave a little scented pillow
To the forgetful one, and he
Returned, returned now wedded.
She died of love.

Ambassadors and bishops
Carried her bier, and there were
Relays of people following,
All with flowers.

. . . Wishing to see him again,
She went out on the belvedere;
He returned with his wife:
She died of love.

Her brow was like molten bronze
At his parting kiss,
The brow I loved the best
In all my life!

. . . At dusk she entered the river;
The doctor pulled out her body.
They say she died of cold; I know
She died of love.

Allí, en la bóveda helada,
La pusieron en dos bancos:
Besé su mano afilada,
Besé sus zapatos blancos.

Callado, al oscurecer,
Me llamó el enterrador:
¡Nunca más he vuelto a ver
A la que murió de amor!

They laid her out on two benches
There in the frigid vault;
I kissed her slender hand
And her white shoes.

Softly, when evening fell,
The gravedigger bid me come.
Never again did I see that girl
Who died of love.

X

El alma trémula y sola
Padece al anochecer:
Hay baile; vamos a ver
La bailarina española.

Han hecho bien en quitar
El banderón de la acera;
Porque si está la bandera,
No sé, yo no puedo entrar.

Ya llega la bailarina:
Soberbia y pálida llega:
¿Cómo dicen que es gallega?
Pues dicen mal: es divina.

Lleva un sombrero torero
Y una capa carmesí:
¡Lo mismo que un alelí
Que se pusiese un sombrero!

Se ve, de paso, la ceja,
Ceja de mora traidora:
Y la mirada, de mora:
Y como nieve la oreja.

Preludian, bajan la luz,
Y sale en bata y mantón,
La virgen de la Asunción
Bailando un baile andaluz.

Alza, retando, la frente:
Crúzase al hombro la manta:
En arco el brazo levanta:
Mueve despacio el pie ardiente.

X

The lonely trembling soul can ache
When night is on the way;
There is a dance: let's go
To see the Spanish dancer.

It's good they took away
The big flag from the sidewalk,
For should it still be there
I doubt if I could enter.

The dancer is arriving now,
Haughty and pale of face;
Why say she is Galician?
Not so; she is divine.

She wears a matador's hat
And a cape of brightest red;
She's like a gilliflower
That had put on a hat!

We notice her brows in passing,
The brows of a traitorous Mooress,
The glance of a Moorish lady,
The ears like driven snow.

A musical flourish, lights dim;
The Virgin of the Assumption
Appears in shawl and gown
In a dance of Andalusia.

She raises her head in challenge,
Draws round her shoulders her shawl,
She arches her arms above her,
Moves slowly her ardent feet.

Repica con los tacones
El tablado zalamera,
Como si la tabla fuera
Tablado de corazones.

Y va el convite creciendo
En las llamas de los ojos,
Y el mantón de flecos rojos
Se va en el aire meciendo.

Súbito, de un salto arranca:
Húrtase, se quiebra, gira:
Abre en dos la cachemira,
Ofrece la bata blanca.

El cuerpo cede y ondea;
La boca abierta provoca;
Es una rose la boca:
Lentamente taconea.

Recoge, de un débil giro,
El manto de flecos rojos:
Se va, cerrando los ojos,
Se va, como en un suspiro . . .

Baile muy bien la española;
Es blanco y rojo el mantón:
¡Vuelve, fosca, a su rincón
El alma trémula y sola!

Fawning, she taps on the stage
With the heels of her shoes as if
The flooring beneath her feet
Were a flooring composed of hearts.

The festive mood is increasing
In the fire of her eyes,
As she waves her red-dotted shawl
Round and round in the air.

She starts with a sudden leap,
Draws back, whirls round, and dips;
She opens her cashmere shawl,
Revealing a snow-white gown.

Her body yields and undulates,
She parts her provocative lips,
Those lips so like a rose,
And leisurely taps her heels.

Feebly turning, she gathers up
Her shawl that is dotted with red,
Then shuts her eyes and departs,
Departs as if in a sigh . . .

The Spanish girl dances well;
Her shawl is scarlet and white;
The lonely trembling soul returns
In a sullen mood to its corner!

XII

En el bote iba remando
Por el lago seductor
Con el sol que era oro puro
Y en el alma más de un sol.

Y a mis pies vi de repente,
Ofendido del hedor,
Un pez muerto, un pez hediondo
En el bote remador.

XII

I went rowing in a boat
Upon a tempting lake,
With a sun of purest gold
And more than a sun in my soul.

Offended by a stench,
I suddenly saw a fish,
A dead and stinking fish
Close beside me in the boat.

XXIII

Yo quiero salir del mundo
Por la puerta natural:
En un carro de hojas verdes
A morir me han de llevar.

No me pongan en lo oscuro
A morir como un traidor:
¡Yo soy bueno, y como bueno
Moriré de cara al sol!

XXIII

I want to leave this world
By the natural door;
They must carry me off to die
In a cart of green leaves.

Do not put me in the dark
To die like a traitor;
I am good, and so I shall die
With my face to the sun!

XXX

El rayo surca, sangriento,
El lóbrego nubarrón:
Echa el barco, ciento a ciento,
Los negros por el portón.

El viento, fiero, quebraba
Los almácigos copudos;
Andaba la hilera, andaba,
De los esclavos desnudos.

El temporal sacudía
Los barracones henchidos:
Una madre con su cría
Pasaba, dando alaridos.

Rojo, como en el desierto,
Salió el sol al horizonte:
Y alumbró a un esclavo muerto,
Colgado a un seibo del monte.

Un niño lo vio: tembló
De pasión por los que gimen:
¡Y, al pie del muerto, juró
Lavar con su vida el crimen!

XXX

Blood-red lightning cleaves
The murky overcast; a ship
Disgorges Negroes by the hundreds
Through the hatches.

The raging winds laid low
the full-leafed mastic trees,
And rows of naked slaves
Walked onward, onward.

The tempest shook
The barracks filled with slaves;
A mother and babe passed by
And both were screaming.

Red as a desert sun
The sun rose at the horizon
And shone upon a dead slave hanged
From a mountain ceiba.

A small boy witnessed it
And trembled for the groaning men;
At the victim's feet he vowed to cleanse
That crime with his life.

XXXII

En el negro callejón
Donde en tinieblas paseo,
Alzo los ojos, y veo
La iglesia, erguida, a un rincón.

¿Será misterio? ?Sera
Revelación y poder?
¿Será, rodilla, el deber
De postrarse? ?Qué será?

Tiembla la noche: en la parra
Muerde el gusano el retoño;
Grazna, llamando al otoño,
La hueca y hosca cigarra.

Graznan dos: atento al dúo
Alzo los ojos y veo
Que la iglesia del paseo
Tiene la forma de un búho.

XXXII

In a pitch dark alley
Where I stroll in darkness,
I raise my eyes and see a church,
Stiff-standing and remote.

Is there some mystery,
Some power or revelation?
Are you obliged, my knee, to genuflect?
I wonder what it is?

Night shimmers; a worm nibbles
At the tendrils of a vine.
Calling to Autumn, the vain and sullen
Cicada sings its song.

A pair is singing: intent on both,
I raise my eyes and see
That the church of my stroll
Has the form of an owl.

XXXIV

¡Penas! ¿Quién osa decir
Que tengo yo penas? Luego,
Después del rayo, y del fuego,
Tendré tiempo de sufrir.

Yo sé de un pesar profundo
Entre las penas sin nombres:
¡La esclavitud de los hombres
Es la gran pena del mundo!

Hay montes, y hay que subir
Los montes altos; ¡después
Veremos, alma, quién es
Quien te me ha puesto al morir!

XXXIV

Sorrows! Who dares to say
That I am sorrowful? Later,
After the lightning and fire,
I'll have the time to grieve.

I know of one great sorrow
Among the nameless ones:
The world's enormous sorrow
Is human slavery!

Mountains exist; the high ones
Must be climbed; and then,
My soul, we'll see
What made me die for you!

XXXVI

Ya sé: de carne se puede
Hacer una flor: se puede,
Con el poder del cariño,
Hacer un cielo,—¡y un niño!

De carne se hace también
El alacrán: y también
El gusano de la rosa,
Y la lechuza espantosa.

XXXVI

I know: from flesh
A flower can be made;
From the power of love,
A sky—and a child!

From flesh a scorpion
Is also made; the worm
On a rose, as well,
And the awesome owl.

XXXIX

Cultivo una rosa blanca
En julio como en enero,
Para el amigo sincero
Que me da su mano franca.

Y para el cruel que me arranca
El corazón con que vivo,
Cardo ni oruga cultivo:
Cultivo la rosa blanca.

XXXIX

I cultivate white roses
In January as in July
For the honest friend who freely
Offers me his hand.

And for the brute who tears from me
The heart with which I live,
I nurture neither grubs nor thistles,
But cultivate white roses.

XLV

Sueño con claustros de mármol
Donde en silencio divino
Los héroes, de pie, reposan:
¡De noche, a la luz del alma,
Hablo con ellos: de noche!
Están en fila: paseo
Entre las filas: las manos
De piedra les beso: abren
Los ojos de piedra: mueven
Los labios de piedra: tiemblan
Las barbas de piedra: empuñan
La espada de piedra: lloran:
¡Vibra la espada en la vaina!
Mudo, les beso la mano.

¡Hablo con ellos, de noche!
Están en fila: paseo
Entre las filas: lloroso
Me abrazo a un mármol: "¡Oh mármol,
Dicen que beben tus hijos
Su propia sangre en las copas
Venenosas de sus dueños!
¡Que hablan la lengua podrida
De sus rufianes! ¡Que comen
Juntos el pan del oprobio,
En la mesa ensangrentada!
¡Que pierden en lengua inútil
El último fuego! ¡Dicen,
Oh mármol, mármol dormido,
Que ya se ha muerto tu raza!"

XLV

I dream of marble cloisters
Where in hallowed silence
The standing heroes rest. At night,
By the light of the soul,
I talk with them: at night!
They stand in rows. I walk
Among the rows, kiss
Their stone hands; their
Stone eyes open; their
Stone lips move; their
Stone chins tremble; they clutch
Their swords of stone; they weep;
Their swords vibrate in the scabbards!
Silently I kiss their hands.

I talk with them, at night!
They stand in rows; I walk
Among the rows and tearfully
Embrace a statue: "Oh marble hero,
They say your sons drink of
Their own blood in the poisoned
Goblets of their masters!
Talk the filthy language
Of their villains! together
Eat the bread of infamy
At the bloodstained table!
Squander the final fire
In useless speeches! Oh marble,
Sleeping marble, they say
Your lineage has perished!"

Echame en tierra de un bote
El héroe que abrazo: me ase
Del cuello: barre la tierra
Con mi cabeza: levanta
El brazo, ¡el brazo le luce
Lo mismo que un sol!: resuena
La piedra: buscan el cinto
Las manos blancas: ¡del soclo
Saltan los hombres de mármol!

The hero I embrace fells me
With his sword, seizes me by
The throat, sweeps the ground
With my head, raises an arm
That bathes him with light
As would a sun! The stone
Resounds: the white hands
Seek their girdles, the marble men
Leap from their niches!

XLVI

Vierte, corazón, tu pena
Donde no se llegue a ver,
Por soberbia, y por no ser
Motivo de pena ajena.

Yo te quiero, verso amigo,
Porque cuando siento el pecho
Ya muy cargado y deshecho,
Parto la carga contigo.

Tú me sufres, tú aposentas
En tu regazo amoroso,
Todo mi amor doloroso,
Todas mis ansias y afrentas.

Tú, porque yo pueda en calma
Amar y hacer bien, consientes
En enturbiar tus corrientes
Con cuanto me agobia el alma.

Tú, porque yo cruce fiero
La tierra, y sin odio, y puro,
Te arrastras, pálido y duro,
Mi amoroso compañero.

Mi vida así se encamina
Al cielo limpia y serena,
Y tú me cargas mi pena
Con tu paciencia divina.

Y porque mi cruel costumbre
De echarme en ti te desvía
De tu dichosa armonía
Y natural mansedumbre;

XLVI

Empty your sufferings, oh heart,
Where nobody can see them,
Because of pride, of being
No reason for another's grief.

I love you, friendly poetry,
For when I feel my heart
So burdened and exhausted,
I share the weight with you.

You tolerate me, shelter
In your devoted lap
All my affronts and hankerings
And all my painful love.

So that in calmness I may
Love and be benevolent, you gladly
Cloud your currents with all
That overwhelms my soul.

So that I bravely cross
The land, devoid of hate and pure,
You creep along, my fond companion,
So pale and obstinate.

Thus is my calm and stainless life
Directed toward the skies; and you,
Divinely patient heart,
Are shouldering my grief.

Because of my cruel habit
Of hastening to you, I turned you
From your happy harmony
And natural gentleness.

Porque mis penas arrojo
Sobre tu seno, y lo azotan,
Y tu corriente alborotan,
Y acá lívido, allá rojo,

Blanco allá como la muerte,
Ora arremetes y ruges,
Ora con el peso crujes
De un dolor más que tú fuerte,

¿Habré, como me aconseja
Un corazón mal nacido,
De dejar en el olvido
A aquel que nunca me deja?

¡Verso, nos hablan de un Dios
Adonde van los difuntos:
Verso, o nos condenan juntos,
O nos salvamos los dos!

Because I cast my griefs
Upon your breast, and they belabor it
And make your currents seethe—
Here red, there livid,

And elsewhere white as death—
Now you attack and bellow, then creak
Beneath the weight of sorrows
More powerful than you,

Must I, as counselled by
A lowborn heart, abandon
To oblivion the one
Who never abandons me?

Oh poetry, they tell us of
A God where go the dead;
We are condemned together, poetry,
Or else we both are saved!

TWO POEMS FROM
LA EDAD DE ORO
(The Age of Gold)

Los dos príncipes

Idea de la poetisa norteamericana Helen Hunt Jackson[1]

El palacio está .de luto
Y en el trono llora el rey,
Y la reina está llorando
Donde no la pueden ver:
En pañuelos de holán fino
Lloran la reina y el rey:
Los señores del palacio
Están llorando también.
Los caballos llevan negro
El penacho y el arnés:
Los caballos no han comido,
Porque no quieren comer:
El laurel del patio grande
Quedó sin hoja esta vez:
Todo el mundo fue al entierro
Con coronas de laurel:
—¡El hijo del rey se ha muerto!
¡Se le ha muerto el hijo al rey!

En los álamos del monte
Tiene su casa el pastor:
La pastora está diciendo
"¿Por qué tiene luz el sol?"
Las ovejas, cabizbajas,
Vienen todas al portón:
¡Una caja larga y honda
Está forrando el pastor!
Entra y sale un perro triste:
Canta allá dentro una voz—
"¡Pajarito, yo estoy loca,
Llévame donde él voló!":
El pastor coge llorando
La pala y el azadón:
Abre en la tierra una fosa:
Echa en la fosa una flor:
—¡Se quedó el pastor sin hijo!
¡Murió el hijo del pastor!

The Two Princes

An idea of the North American poet Helen Hunt Jackson[1]

The palace is draped in mourning,
The king on his throne sheds tears
And the queen is also crying,
Where no one can see her cry.
The king and the queen are weeping
Into kerchiefs of fine batiste,
And the noblemen of the palace
Are also shedding tears.
The horses are harnessed in black,
The trappings and their panaches;
The horses have eaten nothing
For they had no wish to eat.
These days the courtyard laurel
Are shorn of all their leaves,
And everyone went to the funeral
Bringing their laurel wreaths—
The king has lost his son!
The son of the king is dead!

The shepherd's house is set
Among the mountain poplars;
The shepherd's wife is asking:
"Why does the sun shed light?"
The sheep, their heads bowed low,
All come to the inner door
Where the shepherd is lining a coffin,
A long and spacious coffin!
A doleful dog is going
Into and out of the house;
Within a voice is singing:
"I am crazy, my little bird;
Do take me to where he flew!"
The weeping shepherd seizes
His shovel and his hoe;
He digs a grave in the ground
And tosses a flower within.
The shepherd has no son left!
The son of the shepherd is dead!

Los zapaticos de rosa

A mademoiselle Marie: José Martí

Hay sol bueno y mar de espuma,
Y arena fina, y Pilar
Quiere salir a estrenar
Su sombrerito de pluma.

—"¡Vaya la niña divina!"
Dice el padre, y le da un beso:
—"¡Vaya mi pájaro preso
A buscarme arena fina!"

—"Yo voy con mi niña hermosa",
Le dijo la madre buena:
"¡No te manches en la arena
Los zapaticos de rosa!"

Fueron las dos al jardín
Por la calle del laurel:
La madre cogió un clavel
Y Pilar cogió un jazmín.

Ella va de todo juego,
Con aro, y balde y paleta:
El balde es color violeta:
El aro es color de fuego.

Vienen a verlas pasar:
Nadie quiere verlas ir:
La madre se echa a reír,
Y un viejo se echa a llorar.

El aire fresco despeina
A Pilar, que viene y va
Muy oronda: "¡Di, mamá!
¿Tú sabes qué cosa es reina?"

The rose-colored slippers

To Mademoiselle Marie

The sand is fine by the choppy sea,
The sun shines as brightly as fire;
Pilar wants to show off her fine feathered hat
For all to observe and admire.

"An enchanting child," her father says,
And kisses her on the hand.
"Go to the beach, my captive bird,
And bring me some of that sand."

"I'll go with my pretty daughter,"
Pilar's good mother decides.
"But don't let those rose-colored slippers
Get soiled by the sand or the tides!"

So both went out to the garden
By the laurel-bordered way;
The mother plucked a carnation,
Pilar picked a jasmine spray.

Pilar with her gay purple pail,
Her shovel and bright red hoop,
Is ready to play on the beach now
And some of that sand to scoop.

The people crowd round as they leave;
Not a one wants to bid them good-bye;
Then Pilar's *mamá* starts laughing
And an old man begins to cry.

The breezes muss Pilar's neat hair
As she runs to and fro, still quite clean.
"Mama, would you tell me just how it feels
To be and to act like a queen?"

Y por si vuelven de noche
De la orilla de la mar,
Para la madre y Pilar
Manda luego el padre el coche.

Está la playa muy linda:
Todo el mundo está en la playa:
Lleva espejuelos el aya
De la francesa Florinda.

Está Alberto, el militar
Que salió en la procesión
Con tricornio y con bastón,
Echando un bote a la mar.

¡Y qué mala, Magdalena,
Con tantas cintas y lazos,
A la muñeca sin brazos
Enterrándola en la arena!

Conversan allá en las sillas,
Sentadas con los señores,
Las señoras, como flores,
Debajo de las sombrillas.

Pero está con estos modos
Tan serios, muy triste el mar:
¡Lo alegre es allá, al doblar,
En la barranca de todos!

Dicen que suenan las olas
Mejor allá en la barranca,
Y que la arena es muy blanca
Donde están las niñas solas.

Pilar corre a su mamá:
—''¡Mamá, yo voy a ser buena:
Déjame ir sola a la arena:
Allá, tú me ves, allá!''

Pilar's good father has ordered the coach
Just in case the darkness should come
Unawares from over the wide blue sea,
For he wanted them safely home.

The beach is so lovely this afternoon
And everyone seems to be there;
Florinda, the French girl's nursemaid,
Wears her glasses to guard against glare.

The soldier Alberto is there today;
He seems to be off on a spree
With tricorne hat and his walking stick,
As he launches his boat in the sea.

Magdalena is such a naughty girl
With her ribbons and bows so grand,
For she takes her doll without any arms
And buries it deep in the sand!

In beach chairs arranged along the beach
Some couples go chatting for hours;
Beneath their colorful parasols
The ladies resemble flowers.

But those strange ways make the sea quite sad;
Their manners and customs offend;
All the joy is there by the cliffs far away—
Out there with the crowds round the bend.

The waves sleep more soundly, the people claim,
Over there with the crowds, they say,
And the sand is far whiter and finer, too,
Where none but the little girls play.

Pilar runs right back to her mother now:
"Mama, I shall do as I should;
Let me go and play alone in the sand
Over there; you can see, I'll be good!"

—"¡Esta niña caprichosa!
No hay tarde que no me enojes:
Anda, pero no te mojes
Los zapaticos de rosa."

Le llega a los pies la espuma:
Gritan alegres las dos:
Y se va, diciendo adiós
La del sombrero de pluma.

¡Se va allá, donde ¡muy lejos!
Las aguas son más salobres,
Donde se sientan los pobres,
Donde se sientan los viejos!

Se fue la niña a jugar,
La espuma blanca bajó,
Y pasó el tiempo, y pasó
Un águila por el mar.

Y cuando el sol se ponía
Detrás de un monte dorado,
Un sombrerito callado
Por las arenas venía.

Trabaja mucho, trabaja
Para andar: ¿qué es lo que tiene
Pilar, que anda así, que viene
Con la cabecita baja?

Bien sabe la madre hermosa
Por qué le cuesta el andar;
—"¡Y los zapatos, Pilar,
Los zapaticos de rosa?

—"¡Ah, loca! ¿en donde estaran?
¡Di, donde, Pilar" —"Señora"
Dice una mujer que llora:
"¡Están conmigo: aquí están!

"Pilar, you're so very capricious!
Not a day when you don't make me fret!
Go and play, but do not let the water
Get those rose-colored slippers all wet."

The wavelets creep up to their feet
And both of them cry out with glee;
The girl in her feather-trimmed hat
Waves good-bye as she runs by the sea.

She runs off to where, far away,
The waters are heavy with brine,
Away where the poor are relaxing,
Away where the aged spend time!

Pilar goes to play by herself
As the wavelets slip back to their bed,
And time goes by and an eagle
Soars high in the sky overhead.

And quite a while after the sun sank
O'er the golden hills beyond reach,
A modest and small feathered hat
Could be seen coming back o'er the beach.

Pilar walked as if deeply troubled;
Her gait was like one who is lame.
Oh why does that child walk like that,
With her head hanging low and in shame?

Her pretty *mamá* knows full well
Why she walks in that shamefaced way:
"I don't see your rose-colored slippers;
Where are they, my child, do say!

"Oh foolish girl, did you lose them?
Tell me, Pilar," said she.
"Señora," a woman in tears replied,
"I have them right here with me!

—"Yo tengo una niña enferma
Que llora en el cuarto obscuro,
Y la traigo al aire puro
A ver el sol, y a que duerma.

"Anoche soñó, soñó
Con el cielo, y oyó un canto:
Me dio miedo, me dio espanto,
Y la traje, y se durmió.

"Con sus dos brazos menudos
Estaba como abrazando;
Y yo mirando, mirando
Sus piececitos desnudos,

"Me llegó al cuerpo la espuma,
Alcé los ojos, y vi
Esta niña frente a mí
Con su sombrero de pluma.

—"¡Se parece a los retratos
Tu niña!" dijo: "¿Es de cera?
¿Quiere jugar? ¡Si quisiera! . . .
¿Y por qué está sin zapatos?

"Mira: ¡la mano le abrasa,
Y tiene los pies tan fríos!
¡Oh, toma, toma los míos;
Yo tengo más en mi casa!"

"No sé bien, señora hermosa,
Lo que sucedió después:
¡Le vi a mi hijita en los pies
Los zapaticos de rosa!"

Se vio sacar los pañuelos
A una rusa y a una inglesa;
El aya de la francesa
Se quitó los espejuelos.

"I have a sick little daughter
Who cries in her dismal room,
So I carry her here for the sea air
And to sleep in the sun, not the gloom.

"Last night she dreamed about Heaven;
Heard a song, do you understand?
This filled me with fear and foreboding,
So I brought her to sleep on the sand.

"I saw her two tiny arms folded
As if in a close embrace,
And noticed her poor little feet so bare
And the look on her sad little face.

"When the surf crept up to my body,
I looked up and saw your daughter—
Your child with her new feathered hat
As she stood between us and the water.

" 'Your child looks just like a picture;
Is she made out of wax?' asked Pilar.
'And tell me, why has she no shoes on?
Can she play? We will not go too far.

" 'But see, her hands are on fire
And her feet are as frozen as ice!
Oh, take all my things, please do take them;
I have others at home just as nice!'

"After that, pretty lady, what happened
Is something I can't quite recall,
But I saw some rose-colored slippers
On my little girl's feet, that is all!"

Two women—one English, one Russian—
Removed their fine neckerchiefs then;
And Florinda, the French girl's nursemaid,
Removed her eyeglasses again.

Abrió la madre los brazos:
Se echó Pilar en su pecho,
Y sacó el traje deshecho,
Sin adornos y sin lazos.

Todo lo quiere saber
De la enferma la señora:
¡No quiere saber que llora
De pobreza una mujer!

—"¡Sí, Pilar, dáselo! ¡Y eso
También! ¡Tu manta! ¡Tu anillo!"
Y ella le dio su bolsillo:
Le dio el clavel, le dio un beso.

Vuelven calladas de noche
A su casa del jardín:
Y Pilar va en el cojín
De la derecha del coche.

Y dice una mariposa
Que vio desde su rosal
Guardados en un cristal
Los zapaticos de rosa.

The sick girl's *mamá* spread her arms
And enfolded Pilar to her breast,
Unbuttoned her daughter's frayed dress
(Lacking ribbons and bows, though her best).

Now Pilar's *mamá* wants to know
Every detail about the sick child;
She cannot abide to see anyone weep,
To illness and need reconciled.

"Yes, indeed, dear Pilar, you may give them!
Your cloak and your ring—and that too!"
Pilar gave the woman her purse then,
The carnation, a kiss: "They're for you!"

At night they returned in deep silence
To their home with its garden in bloom,
Pilar perched atop a soft cushion
And both with no signs of past gloom.

And a butterfly poised on a rose bush
In a looking glass claimed it observed
A reflection of rose-colored slippers
Held therein and forever preserved.

A Adelaida Baralt

De una novela sin arte

La comisión ahí envío:
¡Bien haya el pecado mío
Ya que a Vd. le deja parte!

Cincuenta y cinco fue el precio:
La quinta es de Vd., la quinta
De cincuenta y cinco, pinta
Once, si yo no soy necio.

Para alivio de desgracias
¡Sea!: de lo que yo no quiero
Aliviarme es del sincero
Deber de darle las gracias.

JOSÉ MARTÍ

To Adelaida Baralt

*Referring to an unskilled novel**

I send you this commission
For a novel with talents few;
I readily accept the blame
Since part remains with you!

The payment comes to fifty-five:
One fifth is yours to keep;
A fifth of fifty-five's eleven
If my brain's not asleep.

May this sum lessen your ill-luck,
But what I don't desire
To lessen is my duty true
To give you thanks entire.

*Martí refers to the novel *Amistad Funesta* (Ill-fated Friendship) which
he published in New York's *El Latino Americano* under the pseudonym
of Adelaida Ral. The magazine's editors commissioned Ms. Adelaida
Baralt to write a novel, but she gave the assignment to Martí.

In the 1964 edition of *Obras Completas* the first stanza has only three
lines. I incorporated the subtitle to keep the rhyme scheme. EDR

VERSOS LIBRES
(Free Verse)

MIS VERSOS

$\acute{E}$STOS son mis versos. Son como son. A nadie los pedí prestados. Mientras no pude encerrar íntegras mis visiones en una forma adecuada a ellas, dejé volar mis visiones: ¡oh, cuánto áureo amigo que ya nunca ha vuelto! Pero la poesía tiene su honradez, y yo he querido siempre ser honrado. Recortar versos, también sé, pero no quiero. Así como cada hombre trae su fisonomía, cada inspiración trae su lenguaje. Amo las sonoridades difíciles, el verso escultórico, vibrante como la porcelana, volador como un ave, ardiente y arrollador como una lengua de lava. El verso ha de ser como una espada reluciente, que deja a los espectadores la memoria de un guerrero que va camino al cielo, y al envainarla en el Sol, se rompe en alas.

Tajos son estos de mis propias entrañas—mis guerreros. —Ninguno me ha salido recalentado, artificioso, recompuesto, de la mente; sino como las lágrimas salen de los ojos y la sangre sale a borbotones de la herida.

No zurcí de éste y aquél, sino sajé en mí mismo. Van escritos, no en tinta de academia, sino en mi propia sangre. Lo que aquí doy a ver lo he visto antes (yo lo he visto, yo), y he visto mucho más, que huyó sin darme tiempo a que copiara sus rasgos. —De la extraneza, singularidad, prisa, amontonamiento, arrebato de mis visiones, yo mismo tuve la culpa, que las he hecho surgir ante mí como las copio. De la copia yo soy el responsable. Hallé quebrados los vestidos, y otros no y usé de estos colores. Ya sé que no son usados. Amo la sonoridades dificiles y la sinceridad, aunque pueda parecer brutal.

Todo lo que han de decir, ya lo sé, y me lo tengo contestado. He querido ser leal, y si pequé, no me avergüenzo de haber pecado.

MY POETRY[1]

*T*HESE are my poems. They are what they are. I have not borrowed them from anyone. As long as I could not lock up my visions whole, and in a form worthy of them, I allowed them to fly. Oh, how many golden friends have never returned! But poetry has its honesty, and I have always wanted to be honest. I also know how to trim my poems, but I do not wish to do so. Just as every man has his own physiognomy, every inspiration has its own language. I love the difficult sonorities, the sculptural line: vibrant as porcelain, swift as a bird, scalding and flowing as a tongue of lava. A poem should be like a shining sword that leaves the spectators with memories of a warrior bound for the heavens; when he sheathes his sword in the sun, it breaks into wings.

These poems—my warriors—are cut out of my very entrails. Not one of them has left my mind artfully or warmed over, but rather as tears leave the eyes and blood bubbles out of a wound.

I have not concocted my poems from any others, but tapped them from within myself. They are not written with academic ink, but with my own blood. That which I am giving you to see here, I have seen before, indeed I have, and I have seen much more that escaped before giving me time to set down their features. I myself am to blame for the strangeness, singularity, haste, rage, and piling up of my visions, for I have made them appear before me as I set them down. I found some garments in tatters, others whole, and made use of their colors. I know they are not fashionable. I love sincerity and the difficult sonorities even if they seem brutal.

I already know everything they have to say, and for myself consider it answered. I have wanted to be loyal, and if I have sinned I am not ashamed.

"Pollice verso"

(Memoria de presidio)

Sí iyo también, desnuda la cabeza
De tocado y cabellos, y al tobillo
Una cadena lurda, heme arrastrado
Entre un montón de sierpes, que revueltas
Sobre sus vicios negros, parecían
Esos gusanos de pesado vientre
Y ojos viscosos, que en hedionda cuba
De pardo lodo lentos se revuelcan!
Y yo pasé, sereno entre los viles,
Cual si en mis manos, como en ruego juntas,
Las anchas alas púdicas, abriese
Una paloma blanca. Y aún me aterro
De ver con el recuerdo lo que he visto
Una vez con mis ojos. Y espantado,
¡Póngome en pie, cual a emprender la fuga!
¿Recuerdos hay que queman la memoria!
¡Zarzal es la memoria; mas la mía
Es un cesto de llamas! A su lumbre
El porvenir de mi nación preveo.
Y lloro. Hay leyes en la mente, leyes
Cual las del río, el mar, la piedra, el astro.
Asperas y fatales: ese almendro
Que con su rama oscura en flor sombrea
Mi alta ventana, viene de semilla
De almendro; y ese rico globo de oro
De dulce y perfumoso jugo lleno
Que en blanca fuente una niñuela cara,
Flor del destierro, cándida me brinda,
Naranja es, y vino de naranjo.
Y el suelo triste en que se siembran lágrimas,
Dará árbol de lágrimas. La culpa
Es madre del castigo. No es la vida
Copa de mago que el capricho torna
En hiel para los míseros, y en férvido
Tokay para el feliz. La vida es grave,
Y hasta el pomo ruin la daga hundida,
Al flojo gladiador clava en la arena.

Prison Recollections

Yes! I too, my head shorn, my ankles
Bound with a heavy chain, have crawled
Among a heap of snakes jumbled
In confusion on their dark vices, looking
Like those heavy-bellied worms with viscous eyes
That wallow slowly in a stinking bucket of brown mud!
I moved serenely among those wretched men
As if between my hands, folded in supplication,
The broad, chaste wings of a white dove
Were spreading. And I am still appalled to see in memory
What once my eyes did see. And terrified,
I rise to my feet as if to venture an escape!
Some memories sear the mind!
The memory is a bramble patch, but mine
Is a basket of flames! In their bright light
I can foresee my nation's future.
And I weep. The mind has laws, laws
Like those of the sea, the stone, the star, the river,
Harsh and fatal. That almond tree
Whose somber branches in full bloom give shade
To my wide balcony, comes from the seed
Of the almond tree. And that delicious golden
Globe bursting with sweet and fragrant juice
Which a dear little girl, a flower of exile,
Presents to me upon a snow-white platter,
Is an orange, wine of the orange tree.
And the sad soil where tears are scattered
Will yield a tree of tears. And guilt
Is the mother of punishment. Life is not
A magic cup capriciously transformed
To gall for the wretched, to fervid
Tokay for the fortunate. Life is grave,
And in the amphitheater the dagger stabs
The weakened gladiator up to its wicked hilt.

¡Alza, oh pueblo, el escudo, porque es grave
Cosa esta vida, y cada acción es culpa
Que como aro servil se lleva luego
Cerrado al cuello, o premio generoso
Que del futuro mal próvido libra!
¿Veis los esclavos? ¡Como cuerpos muertos
Atados en racimo, a vuestra espalda
Irán vida tras vida, y con las frentes
Pálidas y angustiosas, la sombría
Carga en vano halaréis, hasta que el viento,
De vuestra pena bárbara apiadado,
Los átomos postreros evapore!
¡Oh, qué visión tremenda! ¡Oh, qué terrible
Procesión de culpables! Como en llano
Negro los miro, torvos, anhelosos,
Sin fruta el arbolar, secos los píos
Bejucos, por comarca funeraria
¡Donde ni el sol da luz, ni el árbol sombra!
Y bogan en silencio, como en magno
Océano sin agua, y a la frente
Porción del Universo frase unida
A frase colosal, sierva ligada
A un carro de oro, que a los ojos mismos
De los que arrastra en rápida carrera
Ocúltase en el áureo polvo, sierva
Con escondidas riendas ponderosas
A la incansable eternidad atada!

Lift high your shield, oh nation, because this life
Is serious, and every act a guilty one;
For, like the lowly hoop, it presently
Shuts round the neck, or is a lavish prize
That providently sets one free from a bad future.
You see those slaves? Like corpses bound
Together in a heap they will move on, life after life,
Behind your back, with anguished pallid foreheads,
And you will vainly haul the sullen cargo, pulling
Until the wind, a barbarian taking pity on your pain,
Evaporates their final atoms!
Oh what a dreadful vision! Oh what a terrible
Procession of the guilty! I look at them as if
They were upon a dismal plain, sullen and yearning,
The grove bearing no fruit, the merciful *bejucos*
Withered, in a funereal region where
The sun provides no light, the trees no shade!
They row in silence as if upon a spacious ocean
Drained of water, and to the mind
A pittance of the universe, a phrase united
To a colossal phrase, a female slave bound
To a golden car which, to the very eyes
Of those it carries off so rapidly,
Is hidden in the golden dust, a slave
Bound fast with heavy hidden reins
To indefatigable Eternity!

Circo la tierra es, como el romano;
Y junto a cada cuna una invisible
Panoplia al hombre aguarda, donde lucen,
Cual daga cruel que hiere al que la blande,
Los vicios, y cual límpidos escudos
Las virtudes: la vida es la ancha arena,
Y los hombres esclavos gladiadores.
Mas el pueblo y el rey, callados miran
De grada excelsa, en la desierta sombra.
¡Pero miran! Y a aquel que en la contienda
Bajó el escudo, o lo dejó de lado,
O suplicó cobarde, o abrió el pecho
Laxo y servil a la enconosa daga
Del enemigo, las vestales rudas,
Desde el sitial de la implacable piedra,
Condenan a morir, *pollice verso*;
¡Llevan, cual yugo el buey, la cuerda uncida,
Y a la zaga, listado el cuerpo flaco
De hondas azotes, el montón de siervos!

¿Veis las carrozas, las ropillas blancas
Risueñas y ligeras, el luciente
Corcel de crin trenzada y riendas ricas,
Y la albarda de plata suntuosa
Prendida, y el menudo zapatillo
Cárcel a un tiempo de los pies y el alma?
¡Pues ved que los extraños os desdeñan
Como a raza ruin, menguada y floja!

The world is an amphitheater like the Roman;
Beside each cradle an invisible
Panoply waits for man, and from it, like a cruel dagger
That wounds the one who wields it, the vices shine;
And like translucent shields, the virtues.
Life is a vast arena and men the gladiator slaves.
But people and kin watch silently
From a lofty gradin in a deserted shelter.
But they are watching! And he who lowered
His shield in the fight, or put it aside,
Or begged like a coward, or bared his flaccid
Slavish breast to the enemy's rancorous dagger—
That man the unrelenting vestals,
From their implacable stone seats of honor,
Condemn to death, *pollice verso.*
They take the subjugating rope as oxen take the yoke,
And lagging behind, their weakened bodies striped
By merciless lashings, the heap of slaves!

You see the stately carriages, the pleasing
Light-weight doublets, the shining chargers
With braided manes and richly embossed reins,
The sumptuous saddles trimmed
With silver, the little shoes
Imprisoning at once the feet and soul?
See, then, how much the foreigners despise you,
You weak and cowardly and despicable race!

Ganado tengo el pan: hágase el verso,—
Y en su comercio dulce se ejercite
La mano, que cual prófugo perdido
Entre oscuras malezas, o quien lleva
A rastra enorme peso, andaba ha poco
Sumas hilando y revolviendo cifras.
Bardo ¿consejo quieres? Pues descuelga
De la pálida espalda ensangrentada
El arpa dívea, acalla los sollozos
Que a tu garganta como mar en furia
Se agolparán, y en la madera rica
Taja plumillas de escritorio y echa
Las cuerdas rotas al movible viento.

Oh alma! oh alma buena! mal oficio
Tienes!: póstrate, calla, cede, lame
Manos de potentado, ensalza, excusa
Defectos, tenlos —que es mejor manera
De excusarlos—, y mansa y temerosa
Vicios celebra, encumbra vanidades:
Verás entonces, alma, cuál se trueca
En plato de oro rico tu desnudo
Plato de pobre!
                    Pero guarda ¡oh alma!
Que usan los hombres hoy oro empañado!
Ni de eso cures, que fabrican de oro
Sus joyas el bribón y el barbilindo:
Las armas no, —las armas son de hierro!

Mi mal es rudo: la ciudad lo encona:
Lo alivia el campo inmenso: ¡Otro más vasto
Lo aliviará mejor! —Y las oscuras
Tardes me atraen, cual si mi patria fuera
La dilatada sombra.
                    ¡Oh verso amigo;
Muero de soledad, de amor me muero!
No de amores vulgares; estos amores
Envenenan y ofuscan: no es hermosa

Iron

My bread is earned; make poetry,
Exert your hand in its gentle intercourse—
The hand which, like a fugitive lost
In the dark underbrush, or someone
Bearing a mammoth load unwillingly,
Not long ago was adding sums and juggling ciphers.
Bard, do you wish counsel? Then let
The beguiling harp slip from your pale and bleeding
Shoulder, stifle the sobs
That like an angry sea will flock to your throat,
And on the rich wood surface of a desk
Trim the little feather pens and toss
Your broken harpstrings to the blowing winds.

Oh soul, good soul! Yours is a difficult task!
Kneel down, be still, submit, and lick
The sovereign's hands; extol, forgive
Shortcomings, or have them—which is the best way
To forgive them—and, timorous and meek,
Rejoice in wickedness, enshrine the vanities;
Then you shall see, my soul,
Your poor man's empty dish transformed
Into a dish of richest gold!
                                    But be on guard, oh soul,
For men today use tarnished gold!
So pay no heed—the fops and scoundrels
Make their trinkets out of gold,
But not their guns; their guns are made of iron!

My sickness is severe; the city aggravates it;
The vast expanse of country eases it. Another vaster one
Would ease it better! Dark evenings
Draw me to them as if my native land
Were an extended darkness.
                              Oh friendly poetry,
I die of solitude, of love I die! Not
Of vulgar love affairs; those poison
And confuse. The fruit in woman

La fruta en la mujer, sino la estrella.
La tierra ha de ser luz, y todo vivo
Debe en torno de sí dar lumbre de astro.
¡Oh, estas damas de muestra! Oh, estas copas
De carne! Oh, estas siervas, ante el dueno
Que las enjoya o estremece echadas!
¡Te digo, oh verso, que los dientes duelen
De comer de esta carne!

            Es de inefable
Amor del que yo muero, —del muy dulce
Menester de llevar, como se lleva
Un niño tierno en las cuidosas manos,
Cuanto de bello y triste ven mis ojos.

Del sueno, que las fuerzas no repara
Sino de los dichosos, y a los tristes
El duro humor y la fatiga aumenta,
Salto, al Sol, como un ebrio. Con las manos
Mi frente oprimo, y de los turbios ojos
Brota raudal de lágrimas. ¡Y miro
El Sol tan bello y mi desierta alcoba,
Y mi virtud inútil, y las fuerzas
Que cual tropel famélico de hirsutas
Fieras saltan de mí buscando empleo;—
Y el aire hueco palpo, y en el muro
Frío y desnudo el cuerpo vacilante
Apoyo, y en el cráneo estremecido
El agonía flota el pensamiento,
Cual leño de bajel despedazado
Que el mar en furia a la playa ardiente arroja!
¡Sólo las flores del paterno prado
Tienen olor! ¡Sólo las seibas patrias
Del sol amparan! Como en vaga nube
Por suelo extraño se anda; las miradas
Injurias nos parecen, y el Sol mismo,
Más que en grato calor, enciende en ira!
¡No de voces queridas puebla el eco
Los aires de otras tierras: y no vuelan
Del arbolar espeso entre las ramas
Los pálidos espíritus amados!
De carne viva y profanadas frutas
Viven los hombres, — ¡ay! mas el proscripto

Is not beautiful, only the star.
The earth must be illumination, and every living thing
Shed starlight round it! And oh,
These model ladies, these cups
Of flesh, these female serfs before the master
Who gives them jewels and nourishes them as castaways!
I tell you, poetry, partaking of this flesh
Makes the teeth ache!
                              I die from an ineffable
Love, and from the pleasant
Need of taking—as a tender child
Is taken by caring hands—as much of sadness
And beauty as I can see.

From sleep that only replenishes the forces
Of the fortunate, increasing
The weariness and stubborn dispositions of the sad,
I leap to the sun as if inebriated. Pressing
My hands against my forehead, torrents of tears
Pour from my troubled eyes. I see
The sun so beautiful, my empty room, my useless virtue,
The strength which, like a ravenous herd
Of hairy animals, springs out of me to seek employment.
I touch the empty air, lean my unsteady
Body against the cold and naked wall,
And in my trembling skull
Thoughts float in agony
Like timbers from a shattered ship
Cast by an angry sea upon a burning beach!
None but the flowers of the paternal field
Are fragrant! Only one's native ceiba trees
Give shelter from the sun! One goes about
On foreign soil as in a drifting cloud; mere glances
Seem like insults; and the sun itself,
Instead of shedding pleasant warmth, blazes with rage!
Not with fond voices do echoes
People the winds of other lands, nor do pale
Well-loved spirits fly among the branches
Of dense woodlands!
Men live on living flesh and profaned
Fruits, alas! But exiles
Feed upon their very entrails!

De sus entrañas propias se alimenta!
¡Tiranos: desterrad a los que alcanzan
El honor de vuestro odio: ya son muertos!
Valiera más ¡oh bárbaros! que al punto
De arrebatarlos al hogar, hundiera
En lo más hondo de su pecho honrado
Vuestro esbirro más cruel su hoja más dura!
Grato es morir, horrible, vivir muerto.
¡Mas no! ¡mas no! La dicha es una prenda
De compasión de la fortuna al triste
Que no sabe domarla: a sus mejores
Hijos desgracias da Naturaleza:
Fecunda el hierro al llano, el golpe al hierro!

Oppressors, banish those who reach
The honor of your hate; they are already dead!
Far better, oh barbarians, if when
You snatch them from their homes,
Your cruelest bailiff were to plunge his sharpest blade
Into the deepest portions of their honest hearts!
Pleasant it is to die, dreadful to live while dead.
But no! Not so! Happiness is a clement
Gift of fortune to the sad
Who know not how to master it. Nature
Bestows misfortune upon her finest sons:
As iron fructifies the fields,
The forge shapes iron!

Canto de Otoño

Bien: ¡ya lo sé:—La muerte está sentada
A mis umbrales: cautelosa viene,
Porque sus llantos y su amor no apronten
En mi defensa, cuando lejos viven
Padres e hijo.—Al retornar ceñudo
De mi estéril labor, triste y oscura,
Con que a mi casa del invierno abrigo,—
De pie sobre las hojas amarillas,
En la mano fatal la flor del sueño,
La negra toca en alas rematada,
Ávido el rostro,—trémulo la miro
Cada tarde aguardándome a mi puerta.
¡En mi hijo pienso—y de la dama oscura
Huyo sin fuerzas, devorado el pecho
De un frenético amor! Mujer más bella
No hay que la Muerte! Por un beso suyo
Bosques espesos de laureles varios,
Y las adelfas del amor, y el gozo
De remembrarme mis niñeces diera!
. . . Pienso en aquel a quien mi amor culpable
Trajo a vivir, y, sollozando, esquivo
De mi amada los brazos:—mas ya gozo
De la aurora perenne el bien seguro.
Oh, vida, adiós!:—Quien va a morir, va muerto.

¡Oh, duelos con la sombra: Oh, pobladores
Ocultos del espacio: Oh, formidables
Gigantes que a los vivos azorados
Mueven, dirigen, postran, precipitan!
Oh, cónclave de jueces, blandos sólo
A la virtud, que en nube tenebrosa,
En grueso manto de oro recogidos,
Y duros como peña, aguardan torvos
A que al volver de la batalla rindan
—Como el frutal sus frutos—
De sus obras de paz los hombres cuenta,
De sus divinas alas! . . . ¡de los nuevos

Song of Autumn

Indeed I know! Death is seated
At my doorsill; she comes warily
So that her love and weeping cannot marshal forces
In my defense, when parents and son
Live far away. Returning in a surly mood
From the sterile, sad and dismal work
With which I guard my home from winter,
Trembling, I watch her waiting for me
Every evening at my doorway, sad and dismal,
Standing among the yellowed leaves,
The dream flower in her fatal hand,
Her dark hood ending in wings, her face eager.
My thoughts stray to my son, and I escape
The somber lady feebly, my heart devoured
By a frenetic love! No woman is more beautiful
Than Death! For one of her kisses
I would give forests lush with several kinds of laurel,
The rosebay of love, and the pleasure
Of remembering my childhood!
.... I think about the child my guilty love
Brought into life, and tearfully avoid
My lover's arms; but I enjoy
A certain benefit from the perennial dawn.
Farewell, oh life! Whoever is about to die, is dead.

Oh duels with darkness! Oh hidden
Settlers of space! Oh formidable giants
Who drive and lead, who hasten and exhaust
The terror-stricken living!
Oh conclave of judges, indulgent only
With virtue, who in a gloomy company
As obstinate as rocks, and gathered into
Heavy golden robes, wait sternly for the men
Returned from battle to render an account
—As fruit trees render fruit—
Of their peaceful labors,
Their wings divine ... the sapling

Árboles que sembraron, de las tristes
Lágrimas que enjugaron, de las fosas
Que a los tigres y víboras abrieron,
Y de las fortalezas eminentes
Que al amor de los hombres levantaron!
¡Ésta es la dama, el rey, la patria, el premio
Apetecido, la arrogante mora
Que a su brusco señor cautiva espera
Llorando en la desierta barbacana!:
Éste el santo Salem, éste el Sepulcro
De los hombres modernos:—No se vierta
Más sangre que la propia! No se bata
Sino al que odie al amor! Únjanse presto
Soldados del amor los hombres todos:
La tierra entera marcha a la conquista
De este rey y señor, que guarda el cielo!
. . . Viles: ¡El que es traidor a sus deberes,
Muere como un traidor, del golpe propio
De su arma ociosa el pecho atravesado!
Ved que no acaba el drama de la vida
En esta parte oscura! Ved que luego
Tras la losa de mármol o la blanda
Cortina de humo y césped se reanuda
El drama portentoso! ¡y ved, oh viles,
Que los buenos, los tristes, los burlados,
Serán en la otra parte burladores!

Otros de lirio y sangre se alimentan:
¡Yo no! yo no! Los lóbregos espacios
Rasgué desde mi infancia con los tristes
Penetradores ojos: el misterio
En una hora feliz de sueño acaso
De los jueces así, y amé la vida
Porque del doloroso mal me salva
De volverla a vivir. Alegremente
El peso eché del infortunio al hombro:
Porque el que en huelga y regocijo vive
Y huye el dolor, y esquiva las sabrosas
Penas de la virtud,—irá confuso
Del frío y torvo juez a la sentencia,
Cual soldado cobarde que en herrumbre

Trees they planted, the tragic tears
They wiped away, the graves
They dug for snakes and tigers,
The imposing fortresses
They built for the love of men!
This is the king, the fatherland, the lady,
The coveted prize, the haughty Moorish woman,
Captive and weeping, waiting in the deserted barbican
For her stern master!
This is the sacred Salem, this the Sepulcher
Of modern men. The only bloodshed should be
One's own! Let beatings be reserved
For those who despise love! Soldiers of love,
Anoint all men quickly!
The whole world marches to the conquest of
This lord and king who guards the heavens!
. . . . Abominable ones! A man who shirks his duty
Dies like a traitor, his heart pierced through,
And from the thrust of his own idle sword!
See how life's drama never ends
In these dark parts! See how,
Beyond the marble tombstone or soft curtain
Of vanity and turf, the wondrous drama
Presently resumes again! And see, oh despicable ones,
How upright men, the ridiculed, the sad,
Will be the scoffers elsewhere!

Let others feed on blood and lilies;
Not I! Not I! With sad and penetrating eyes
I have been rending the murky spaces
Since childhood: perhaps while dreaming
In some happy hour, I grasped
The mystery of the judges, and I loved life
Because it spares me from the painful
Malady of living it again. With joy
I threw upon my back the weight of suffering;
For he who lives in joy and idleness,
And flees from sorrow, and shuns the pleasant
Griefs of virtue, will go bewildered
From the cold stern judge to judgment
Like the cowardly soldier who left

Dejó las nobles armas; ¡y los jueces
No en su dosel lo ampararán, no en brazos
Lo encumbrarán, mas lo echarán altivos
A odiar, a amar y batallar de nuevo
En la fogosa sofocante arena!
Oh! qué mortal que se asomó a la vida
Vivir de nuevo quiere? . . .
                                        Puede ansiosa
La Muerte, pues, de pie en las hojas secas,
Esperarme a mi umbral con cada turbia
Tarde de otoño, y silenciosa puede
Irme tejiendo con helados copos
Mi manto funeral.
                            No di al olvido
Las armas del amor: no de otra púrpura
Vestí que de mi sangre. Abre los brazos,
Listo estoy, madre Muerte: al juez me lleva!

Hijo! . . . Qué imagen miro? ¿qué llorosa
Visión rompe la sombra, y blandamente
Como con luz de estrella la ilumina?
¡Hijo! . . . ¿qué me demandan tus abiertos
Brazos? ¿A qué descubres tu afligido
Pecho? ¿Por qué me muestras tus desnudos
Pies, aún no heridos, y las blancas manos
Vuelves a mí, tristísimo gimiendo? . . .
¡Cesa, calla, reposa, vive!: El padre
No ha de morir hasta que a la ardua lucha
Rico de todas armas lance al hijo!—
¡Ven, oh mi hijuelo, y que tus alas blancas
De los abrazos de la Muerte oscura
Y de su manto funeral me libren!

His noble arms to rust. No judges
Will protect him with their canopy, nor lift him
In their arms, but arrogantly send him forth
To hate, to love, and battle once again
In the stifling, fiery arena!
What mortal man born to this life
Would want to live again . . . ?

                              Death, then,
Standing among the withered leaves,
Can eagerly await me at my doorsill
Every murky Autumn evening, and silently
Approach me, weaving with frozen flaxen threads
My winding sheet.

                    I never cast the guns of love
Into oblivion, nor clothed myself in purple
Other than my blood. Spread wide your arms,
Death Mother, I am ready: take me to the judge!

My son. . . ! What image do I see? What tearful
Vision cleaves the darkness, and softly
Illumines it as if with starlight?
My son . . . ! What do your outstretched arms demand
Of me? Why do you bare your anguished
Breast? Why show to me your naked feet,
As yet unwounded, and turn to me your pallid hands
While moaning piteously. . . ?
Desist! Be still! Repose! And live! A father
Must never die until he hurls his son, richly supplied
With every kind of weapon, into the arduous fight!
Come, my little son, and may your unstained wings
Free me from somber Death's embrace
And from her shroud!

                                  New York, 1882

Medianoche

Oh, qué vergüenza!:—El sol ha iluminado
La tierra; el amplio mar en sus entrañas
Nuevas columnas a sus naves rojas
Ha levantado: el monte, granos nuevos
Juntó en el curso del solemne día
A sus jaspes y breñas; en el vientre
De las aves y bestias nuevos hijos
Vida, que es forma, cobran: en las ramas
Las frutas de los árboles maduran:—
¡Y yo, mozo de gleba, he puesto sólo,
Mientras que el mundo gigantesco crece,
Mi jornal en las ollas de la casa!

¡Por Dios, que soy un vil!:—¡No en vano el sueño
A mis pálidos ojos es negado!
¡No en vano por las calles titubeo
Ebrio de un vino amargo, cual quien busca
Fosa ignorada donde hundirse, y nadie
Su crimen grande y su ignominia sepa!
¡No en vano el corazón me tiembla ansioso
Como el pecho sin calma de un malvado!

¡El cielo, el cielo, con sus ojos de oro
Me mira, y ve mi cobardía, y lanza
Mi cuerpo fugitivo por la sombra
Como quien loco y desolado huye
De un vigilante que en sí mismo lleva!
¡La tierra es soledad! ¡La luz se enfría!
¿Adónde iré que este volcan se apague?
¿Adónde iré que el vigilante duerma?

Midnight

For shame! The sun has lighted
The earth; down in its depths the spacious sea has raised
New columns to its scarlet ships; during the solemn day
The woods have added new seed to their craggy ground and jasper.
In the wombs of birds and beasts new young
Are given life, which is form; on branches
Of trees the fruit is ripening. And I,
Young plowboy, while the huge world is growing,
Have merely put my daily wages in the stewpot!

Heavens, how despicable I am! No wonder
My pale eyes can find no sleep!
No wonder that I stagger through the streets,
Reeling from sour wine like someone seeking
An unknown grave to hide in, so nobody
Will know about his infamy or his great crime!
No wonder my heart beats anxiously
Like a villain's troubled heart!

The sky, the sky is watching me
With golden eyes; it sees my cowardice and hurls
My fleeing body through the gloom
Like someone, mad and despairing, escaping
From a watchman he bears within himself!
The earth is solitude! The light grows cold!
Where can I go to burn out this volcano?
Where can I go to let the watchman sleep?

¡Oh, sed de amor! oh, corazon prendado
De cuanto vivo el Universo habita:
Del gusanillo verde en que se trueca
La hoja del árbol:—del rizado jaspe
En que las ondas de la mar se cuajan:—
De los árboles presos, que a los ojos
Me sacan siempre lágrimas;—del lindo
Bribón gentil que con los pies desnudos
En fango y nieve, diario o flor pregona.

¡Oh, corazón, que en el carnal vestido
No hierros de hacer oro, ni belfudos
Labios glotones y sensuosos mira,
Sino corazas de batalla, y hornos
Donde la vida universal fermenta!

Y yo, pobre de mí!, preso en mi jaula,
La gran batalla de los hombres miro!

Oh thirst for love! Oh heart concerned
With every living thing inhabiting the Universe:
A leaf transformed into a small green worm,
The rippled jasper solidified in ocean waves,
Imprisoned trees that always draw
Tears from my eyes, the handsome graceful rogue who hawks
His newspapers or flowers, barefoot in mud and snow.

Oh heart attired in flesh, you do not look
At tools for making gold, or at thick-hanging, sensuous
Greedy lips; you look at battle cuirasses
And vats where universal life ferments.

And I, poor soul, imprisoned in my cage,
Am watching man's great battle!

Yugo y estrella

Cuando nací, sin sol, mi madre dijo:
"—Flor de mi seno, Homagno generoso,
De mí y de la Creación suma y reflejo,
Pez que en ave y corcel y hombre se torna,
Mira estas dos, que con dolor te brindo,
Insignias de la vida: ve y escoge.
Éste, es un yugo: quien lo acepta, goza:
Hace de manso buey, y como presta
Servicio a los señores, duerme en paja
Caliente, y tiene rica y ancha avena.
Ésta, oh misterio que de mí naciste
Cual la cumbre nació de la montaña,
Ésta, que alumbra y mata, es una estrella:
Como que riega luz, los pecadores
Huyen de quien la lleva, y en la vida,
Cual un monstruo de crímenes cargado,
Todo el que lleva luz, se queda solo.
Pero el hombre que al buey sin pena imita,
Buey vuelve a ser, y en apagado bruto
La escala universal de nuevo empieza.
El que la estrella sin temor se ciñe,
Como que crea, ¡crece!:
                            ¡Cuando al mundo
De su copa el licor vació ya el vivo:
Cuando, para manjar de la sangrienta
Fiesta humana, sacó contento y grave
Su propio corazón: cuando a los vientos
De Norte y Sur virtió su voz sagrada,—
La estrella como un manto, en luz lo envuelve,
Se enciende, como a fiesta, el aire claro,
Y el vivo que a vivir no tuvo miedo,
Se oye que un paso más sube en la sombra!"

—Dame el yugo, oh mi madre, de manera
Que puesto en él de pie, luzca en mi frente
Mejor la estrella que ilumina y mata.

Yoke and Star

When I was born, without the sun, my mother said:
"Flower of my womb, noble *Homagno*,
Sum and reflection of me and of Creation,
Fish that becomes a bird, a charger, and a man,
Look at these two insignia of life I offer you
In pain; consider them and choose.
This is a yoke; he who accepts it enjoys,
Acts like a gentle ox, and when he lends his services
To gentlemen, sleeps on warm straw
And eats delicious, full-grained oats.
This one, oh mystery born of me
Like a mountain peak from a mountain—
This one, that lights and kills, is a star.
Because it sheds its brilliance, sinners
Flee from those who wear it, and in this life
All those who wear the light remain alone
Like monsters burdened by crimes.
But he who easily imitates an ox
Becomes one, and once again starts up the universal
Ladder like a submissive beast.
He who bravely girds himself with the star,
Since he creates, he grows!
      When the living one
Empties his cup of liquor on the world;
When, to feed upon the bloody
Human feast, he gravely and contentedly tears out
His very heart, and casts his sacred word
To the North wind and the South,
The star envelops him with light as with a cloak,
The limpid air burns bright as at some festival,
And the living one who has no fear of living
Is heard to climb another step into the dark!"

Give me the yoke, oh Mother, so when I firmly
Stand upon it, the star that lights and kills
May better shine forth from my countenance.

Copa con alas

Una copa con alas: quién la ha visto
Antes que yo? Yo ayer la vi. Subía
Con lenta majestad, como quien vierte
Óleo sagrado: y a sus dulces bordes
Mis regalados labios apretaba:—
¡Ni una gota siquiera, ni una gota
Del bálsamo perdí que hubo en tu beso!

Tu cabeza de negra cabellera
—¿Te acuerdas?—con mi mano requería,
Porque de mí tus labios generosos
No se apartaran.—Blanda como el beso
Que a ti me transfundía, era la suave
Atmósfera en redor: ¡la vida entera
Sentí que a mí abrazándote, abrazaba!
¡Perdí el mundo de vista, y sus ruidos,
Y su envidiosa y bárbara batalla!
Una copa en los aires ascendía,
¡Y yo, en brazos no vistos reclinado
Tras ella, asido de sus dulces bordes,
Por el espacio azul me remontaba!—

¡Oh amor, oh inmenso, oh acabado artista!:
En rueda o riel funde el herrero el hierro:
Una flor o mujer o águila o ángel
En oro o plata el joyador cincela:
¡Tú sólo, sólo tú, sabes el modo
De redudir el Universo a un beso!

The Winged Goblet

A winged goblet, who else besides myself
Has seen it? I saw it yesterday. It rose
With measured majesty as if dispensing
Holy oil; and to its fragrant rim
I pressed my regaled lips.
I lost no drop, no single drop
Of the balsam in your kiss!

My hand caressed your sable hair, remember?
So your inviting lips would not
Leave mine. Soft as the kiss
Transmitting me to you was the soft
Air around us; embracing you
I felt all life embracing me!
I lost sight of the world, its raucous
Sounds and barbarous, envious struggles!
A goblet rose into the air,
And I, in unseen arms reclining
In its wake, seized by its fragrant rim,
And soaring through blue spaces!

Oh love, immense and finished artist!
The blacksmith shapes his iron into rails or wheels;
Jewelers engrave a flower or a woman,
An eagle or an angel, in gold or silver;
But you alone, no one but you, know how
To shrink the universe to a kiss!

Árbol de mi alma

Como un ave que cruza el aire claro,
Siento hacia mí venir tu pensamiento
Y acá en mi corazón hacer su nido.
Ábrese el alma en flor: tiemblan sus ramas
Como los labios frescos de un mancebo
En su primer abrazo a una hermosura.
Cuchichean las hojas: tal parecen
Lenguaraces obreras y envidiosas,
A la doncella de la casa rica
En preparar el tálamo ocupadas.
Ancho es mi corazón, y es todo tuyo.
¡Todo lo triste cabe en el, y todo
Cuanto en el mundo llora, y sufre, y muere!
De hojas secas, y polvo, y derruidas
Ramas lo limpio: bruño con cuidado
Cada hoja, y los tallos: de las flores
Los gusanos y el pétalo comido
Separo: oreo el césped en contorno
Y a recibirte, oh pájaro sin mancha
¡Apresto el corazon enajenado!

Like a bird that flies through cloudless air,
I feel your thoughts coming to me
And building their nests here in my heart.
My soul bursts into bloom; its branches tremble
Like the ruddy lips of a youth
When first embracing beauty.
The leaves are whispering; so appear
Bold-mouthed and envious working women,
Busy preparing the bridal chamber
For the daughter of a wealthy home.
My heart is spacious, and all of it is yours.
All sadness can find room there, and all
In the world that weeps and dies!
I cleanse the world of withered leaves and dust and broken
Branches, carefully polish every leaf and stem,
Remove all worms and moldering petals
From the blooms, refresh the grass around them,
And to welcome you, oh stainless bird,
Prepare my enraptured heart!

Crin hirsuta

Que como crin hirsuta de espantado
Caballo que en los secos troncos mira
Garras y dientes de tremendo lobo,
Mi destrozado verso se levanta? . . .
Sí, pero ¡se levanta!—a la manera
Como cuando el puñal se hunde en el cuello
De la res, sube al cielo hilo de sangre:—
Solo el amor engendra melodías.

The bristling mane

My poetry destroyed—does it rise up
Like the bristling mane of a frightened
Horse that sees the claws and fangs
Of a dreaded wolf beside a dry tree trunk . . . ?
Indeed it does! As when a dagger
Plunges into the neck of a steer,
It rises skyward in a slender thread of blood.
Only love engenders melodies.

FLORES DEL DESTIERRO
(Flowers of Exile)

*E*STAS que ofrezco, no son composiciones acabadas: son, !ay de mí! notas de imágenes tomadas al vuelo, y como para que no se escapasen, entre la muchedumbre antiática de las calles, entre el rodar estruendoso y arrebatado de los ferrocariles, o en los quehaceres apremiantes e inflexibles de un escritorio de comercio—refugio cariñoso del proscripto.

Por qué las publico, no sé: tengo un miedo pueril de no publicarlas ahora. Yo desdeño todo lo mío: y a estos versos, atormentados y rebeldes, sombríos y querellosos, los mimo, y los amo.

Otras cosas podría hacer: acaso no las hago, no las intento acaso, robando horas al sueño, únicas horas mías, porque me parece la expresión la hembra del acto, y mientras hay qué hacer, me parece la mera expresión indigno empleo de fuerzas del hombre. Cada día, de tanta imágen que viene a azotarme las sienes, y a pasearse, como buscando forma, ante mis ojos, pudiera hacer un tomo come este, ¡pero el buey no ara con el arpa de David, que haría sonora la tierra, sino con el arado, que no es lira! ¡Y se van las imágenes, llorosas y torvas, desvanecidas como el humo: y yo me quedo, congojoso y triste, como quien ha faltado a su deber o no ha hecho bien los honores de la visita a una dama benévola y hermosa: y a mis solas, y donde nadie lo sospeche, y sin lágrimas, lloro.

De estos tormentos nace, y con ellos se excusa, este libro de versos.

¡Pudiera surgir de él, como debiera surgir de toda vida, rumbo a la muerte consoladora, un águila blanca!

Ya sé que están escritos en ritmo desusado, que por esto, o por serlo de veras, va a parecer a muchos duro. ¿Mas, con qué derecho puede quebrar la mera voluntad artística,[1] la forma natural y sagrada, en que, como la carne de la idea, envía el alma los versos a los labios? Ciertos versos pueden hacerse en toda forma: otros, no. A cada estado de alma, un metro

---

Aquí aparecen, en el original, varias palabras ininteligibles.

FLOWERS OF EXILE

*T*HESE offerings are not finished compositions; they are, woe is me! notes on some images taken in flight—and as if to prevent their escape—among the inelegant street crowds, the reckless and noisy running of railroad trains, or the pressing and inflexible tasks at an office desk, fond refuge of exiles.

Why I publish them I do not know; I have a childish fear of not publishing them now. I feel contempt for everything of mine, but these anguished, rebellious sullen and querulous poems I indulge and love.

I could do other things, but perhaps I do not do them or even attempt them—robbing hours from sleep, the only hours I have—because I consider expression the female side of action, and while there is something to be done, I feel that mere expression is an unworthy use of man's forces. With so many images coming to strike me in the temples, and wandering about before my eyes as if in quest of form, I might write a volume such as this every day, but an ox does not plow with David's harp, which would make the earth sing; it uses a plow, which is not a lyre! So the images escape, grim, sorrowful, and vanishing like smoke, and I am left distressed and saddened like someone who has shirked his duty or failed to acquit himself well when visiting a kind and beautiful lady. And all alone, where no one suspects it, I weep inwardly.

This book of poetry comes into being because of these torments, and they are its excuse.

A white eagle might emerge from it, as it ought to emerge from every life, bound for a comforting death!

I know that these poems are written in an obsolete meter; for this reason, or because they are truly out of date, many people will consider them harsh. But by what right can mere artistic will* break the natural and

---

*Several unintelligible words here (Editorial Nacional de Cuba)

nuevo. Da el amor versos claros y sonoros, y no sé por qué, en esas horas de florescencia, vertimiento, grata congoja, vigor pujante y generoso rebose del espíritu, recuerdo esas gallardas velas blancas que en el mar sereno cruzan por frente a playas limpias bajo un cielo bruñido. Del dolor, saltan los versos, como las espadas de la vaina, cuando las sacude en ellas la ira, como las negras olas de turbia y alta cresta que azotan los ijares fatigados de un buque formidable en horas de tormenta.

Se encabritan los versos, como las olas: se rompen con fragor o se mueven pesadamente, como fieras en jaula y con indómito y trágico desorden, como las aguas contra el barco. Y parece como que se escapa de los versos, escondiendo sus heridas, un alma sombría, que asciende velozmente por el lúgubre espacio, envuelta en ropas negras. ¡Cuán extraño que se abrieran las negras vestiduras y cayera de ellas un ramo de rosas!

¡Flores del destierro!

sacred form in which, as the essence of an idea, the soul sends poetry to the lips? Certain poems may be composed in any kind of form, others may not. For every state of mind, a new meter. Love gives clear and sonorous lines of poetry, and in these times of florescence, effusion, grateful anguish, eager strength, and noble overflowing of spirit, I do not know why I should remember those gallant white ships that sail calm seas past clean beaches under a burnished sky. Poetry springs from sorrow like swords from their scabbards when anger sets them quivering, or like dark and turbulent high-crested waves that lash the weary gunwales of a formidable ship in stormy weather.

Lines of poetry rear like waves; they shatter noisily or move heavily like wild beasts in a cage, and in untamable and tragic disorder like seas slapping against a ship's hull. It seems as if a somber spirit, clothed in black and swiftly ascending through lugubrious space, were hiding its wounds and escaping from the poetry. How strange that those dark garments should fly open and release a bouquet of roses!

Flowers of exile!

Contra el verso retórico ...

Contra el verso retórico y ornado
El verso natural. Acá un torrente:
Aquí una piedra seca. Allá un dorado
Pájaro, que en las ramas verdes brilla,
Como una marañuela entre esmeraldas—
Acá la huella fétida y viscosa
De un gusano: los ojos, dos burbujas
De fango, pardo el vientre, craso, inmundo.
Por sobre el árbol, más arriba, sola
En el cielo de acero una segura
Estrella; y a los pies el horno,
El horno a cuyo ardor la tierra cuece—
Llamas, llamas que luchan, con abiertos
Huecos como ojos, lenguas como brazos,
Savia como de hombre, punta aguda
Cual de espada: ¡la espada de la vida
Que incendio a incendio gana al fin, la tierra!
Trepa: viene de adentro: ruge: aborta.
Empieza el hombre en fuego y para en ala.
Y a su paso triunfal, los maculados,
Los viles, los cobardes, los vencidos,
Como serpientes, como gozques, como
Cocodrilos de doble dentadura,
De acá, de allá, del árbol que le ampara,
Del suelo que le tiene, del arroyo
Donde apaga la sed, del yunque mismo
Donde se forja el pan, le ladran y echan
El diente al pie, al rostro el polvo y lodo,
Cuanto cegarle puede en su camino.
Él, de un golpe de ala, barre el mundo
Y sube por la atmósfera encendida
Muerto como hombre y como sol sereno.
Así ha de ser la noble poesía:
Así como la vida: estrella y gozque;
La cueva dentellada por el fuego,
El pino en cuyas ramas olorosas
A la luz de la luna canta un nido
Canta un nido a lumbre de la luna.

The opposite of ornate and rhetorical poetry

The opposite of ornate and rhetorical poetry
Is natural poetry. Here a torrent,
There an arid stone, here a golden
Bird that gleams among the verdant branches
Like a nasturtium among emeralds.
There the fetid viscous traces
Of a worm, its eyes two bubbles
Of mire, its belly brownish, gross and filthy.
Above the tree, far higher and alone
In a steel-gray sky, a constant
Star; and down below the star a furnace,
A furnace in whose fires the earth is cooking—
And flames, the flames that struggle, with open
Holes for eyes, their tongues like arms,
Their sap like a man's blood, their sharpened
Points like swords: the swords of life that finally,
From fire to fire, acquire the earth!
The fire climbs, comes from within; it howls, aborts.
Man starts in fire and stops in wings.
At his triumphant step the sullied
And vile, the cowards, the defeated—
Like snakes or mongrels, like
Crocodiles with powerful teeth,
From here, from there, from trees that shelter him,
From lands that hold him, the brooks
That slake his thirst, the very anvil
Where his bread is forged—they bark at him,
Nip at his feet, throw mud and dust in his face,
And all that blinds him on his journey.
But beating his wings he sweeps the world
And rises through the fiery air
Dead as a man, but like a sun serene.
This is what noble poetry should be:
Just as is life: both star and mongrel:
A cave serrated by fire,
A pine tree in whose fragrant branches
A nest of birds sings in the moonlight:
Birds singing in the moonlight.

Dos patrias

Dos patrias tengo yo: Cuba y la noche.
¿O son una las dos? No bien retira
Su majestad el sol, con largos velos
Y un clavel en la mano, silenciosa
Cuba cual viuda triste me aparece.
¡Yo sé cuál es ese clavel sangriento
Que en la mano le tiembla! Está vacío
Mi pecho, destrozado está y vacío
En donde estaba el corazón. Ya es hora
De empezar a morir. La noche es buena
Para decir adiós. La luz estorba
Y la palabra humana. El universo
Habla mejor que el hombre.
                              Cual bandera
Que invita a batallar, la llama roja
De la vela flamea. Las ventanas
Abro, ya estrecho en mí. Muda, rompiendo
Las hojas del clavel, como una nube
Que enturbia el cielo, Cuba, viuda, pasa . . .

Two countries

I have two countries: Cuba and the night.
Or are both one? No sooner does the sun
Withdraw its majesty, than Cuba,
With long veils and holding a carnation,
Appears as a sad and silent widow.
I know about that bloodstained carnation
That trembles in her hand! My breast
Is empty, destroyed and empty
Where the heart lay. Now is the time
To commence dying. Night is a good time
To say farewell. Light is a hindrance
As is the human word. The universe
Talks better than man.
                    Like a flag
That calls to battle, the candle's
Red flame flutters. I feel a closeness
And open windows. Crushing the carnation's
Petals silently, widowed Cuba passes by
Like a cloud that dims the heavens. . . .

Al extranjero

Hoja tras hoja de papel consumo:
Rasgos, consejos, iras, letras fieras
Que parecen espadas: Lo que escribo,
Por compasión lo borro, porque el crimen,
El crimen es al fin de mis hermanos.
Huyo de mí, tiemblo del sol; quisiera
Saber dónde hace el topo su guarida,
Dónde oculta su escama la serpiente,
Dónde sueltan la carga los traidores,
Y dónde no hay honor, sino ceniza:
¡Allí, mas sólo allí, decir pudiera
Lo que dicen y viven!, ¡que mi patria
Piensa en unirse al bárbaro extranjero!

To the foreigner

I destroy sheet after sheet of paper:
Pen strokes, advice, rages, and wild letters
That look like swords. The things I write
I erase out of compassion, because the crime,
The crime is, after all, my brothers'.
I run away from me, shake from the sun. I'd like
To know where moles dig their burrows,
Where snakes hide their scales,
Where traitors throw down their burdens,
And where there is no honor, only ashes.
There, but only there, I might be able to say
What they are saying and living: my country
Intends to join the barbarous foreigner!

Quieren, ¡oh mi dolor!...

Quieren, ¡oh mi dolor!, que a tu hermosura
De su ornamento natural despoje,
Que el árbol pode, que la flor deshoje,
Que haga al manto viril broche y cintura:

Quieren que el verso arrebatado en dura
Cárcel sonante y apretada aherroje,
Cual la espiga deshecha en la alta troje
O en el tosco lagar la vid madura.

No puede ser: la cómica alquilada
El paso ensaye y el sollozo, en donde
Llena de untos, finge que implora:

El gran dolor, el alma desolada,
Ni con carmín su lividez esconde,
Ni se trenza el cabello cuando llora.

Oh woe is me, they want...!

Oh woe is me, they want me to rob your beauty
Of its natural gifts, want me to prune the tree,
To strip the flower of its petals, to make
The manly cloak with a brooch and waistline.

They want me to shackle the impetuous poem
In a cruel, confining, noisy prison,
Like wheat heads spoiled in a tall granary
Or ripe grapes in a rough winepress.

It cannot be: let the hired actress
Rehearse her act and the sob with which,
Covered in greasepaint, she feigns entreaty:

Her great affliction, her desolate soul,
Cannot conceal her lividness with carmine,
Nor can her hair be braided while she weeps.

Bien: yo respeto

Bien: yo respeto
A mi modo brutal, un modo manso
Para los infelices e implacable
Con los que el hambre y el dolor desdeñan,
Y el sublime trabajo; yo respeto
La arruga, el callo, la joroba, la hosca
Y flaca palidez de los que sufren.
Respeto a la infeliz mujer de Italia,
Pura como su cielo, que en la esquina
De la casa sin sol donde devoro
Mis ansias de belleza, vende humilde
Piñas dulces y pálidas manzanas.
Respeto al buen francés, bravo, robusto,
Rojo como su vino, que con luces
De bandera en los ojos, pasa en busca
De pan y gloria al Istmo donde muere.

Indeed, I respect

Indeed: I respect
In my own brutal way, a gentle way
For the unhappy, an implacable way with those
Who are contemptuous of pain and hunger
And of exalted work; respect
The wrinkle, callous, hump, the sullen
Feeble pallor of those who suffer;
Respect the cheerless woman of Italy,
Pure as her sky, who, in a corner
Of the sunless house where I devour
My eagerness for beauty, humbly
Peddles her pale apples and sweet pineapples;
Respect the honest Frenchman, virile, strong,
And ruddy as his wine, who, with the light
Of the flag in his eyes, goes to the Isthmus
In quest of bread and glory, and dies there.

NOTES

Ismaelillo

1. This collection of Martí's poems was published in New York in 1882 by the Thompson and Moreau Press, 51 and 53 Maiden Lane.

Simple Poetry

1. Martí is referring to the defeat of Mexico by the United States in the war fought against Mexico between April, 1846 and September, 1847.
2. Narciso López (1798–1851), born in Venezuela, became a General in the Spanish Army, and married a Cuban. López led a filibustering expedition to liberate Cuba from Spain, was captured by the Spaniards and garrotted. Although he has been viewed as a fighter for the independence of Cuba by some, Martí correctly judged him an annexationist who was linked with Southern slaveholders in a plan to annex Cuba to the United States.
3. William Walker (1824–1862), lawyer at New Orleans who led an armed expedition to Mexico, proclaimed Lower California a republic and himself president in 1853, but was forced out by the Mexican army. He invaded Nicaragua with an army and set up control of the country with the aim of making it part of a Slave Empire with Cuba to be part of the Empire. He was eventually defeated and executed.
4. These verses were published in a small volume in New York City in 1891 by the printer Louis Weiss & Co., 116 Fulton Street.

Two Poems from the *Age of Gold*

LOS DOS PRINCIPES

1. Helen Hunt Jackson (1830–1885), poet and writer, whose concern with justice for the Indian aroused Martí's great admiration. She was the author of two distinguished works: *A Century of Dishonor* (1881), which discussed the many treaties made by the United States in their dealings with Indians (and broken when it it suited the interests of the whites), and the novel *Ramona* (1884), which offers a more personalized version of the tragic relationship of the Indian to the white Americans. Martí translated *Ramona* into Spanish.

FREE VERSE

1. On the margin of Martí's manuscript of his *Free Verses* there is this scarcely legible note, written in pencil: "I wrote these lines when I was twenty-five; today I am forty. To renew poetic form, one must write a living poetry, honestly expressing one's free thought."

   This would indicate that these poems were written in 1878, yet many are signed with the year 1882 in Martí's own handwriting.

2. For a prose presentation by Martí of his prison experience, see *Our America*, pp. 151-89.

LATIN AMERICA IN ITS CULTURE SERIES

LATIN AMERICA IN ITS LITERATURE

General Editor: Cesar Fernandez Moreno
Assistant Editor: Julio Ortega
Edited with an introduction for the English-language edition by
Ivan A. Schulman
Translated from the Spanish by
Mary G. Berg

The richness and vibrancy of modern Latin American literature is examined here by distinguished critics and writers. Though the points of view are diverse, collectively they demonstrate the complex relationship between literature and social reality. Separate sections deal with such themes as ruptures with tradition, experimentation in literature, the liberalization of literary language, and the social function of literature. The significance, for both Latin American and world literature, of such internationally acclaimed writers as Miguel Angel Asturias, Jorge Luis Borges, Gabriel García Márquez, Pablo Neruda, Octavio Paz, and Mario Vargas Llosa is carefully considered.

CONTENTS

Cultural Plurality: G. R. *Coulthard* • Unity and Diversity: *J. L. Martínez* • Tradition and Renewal: *E. Rodríguez Monegal* • The Baroque and the Neobaroque: *S. Sarduy* • Crisis of Realism: *R. Xirau* • Destruction and Forms in Fiction: *N. Jitrik* • Antiliterature: *F. Alegría* • The New Criticism: *F. Sucre* • Beyond Exclusive Languages: *H. de Campos* • Intercommunication and the New Literature: *R. Fernández Retamar* • Literature and Underdevelopment: *A Cândido* • Literature and Society: *J. A. Portuondo* • A Permanent Discussion: *J. M. Oviedo* • Image of Latin America: *J. Lezama Lima*

356 pp. / bibliography, index/ ISBN 0-8419-0530-4 / 1980
$44.50

LATIN AMERICA IN ITS ARCHITECTURE

Edited by Roberto Segre
Edited with an introduction for the English-
language edition by
Fernando Kusnětzoff
Translated from the Spanish by
Edith Grossman

Architecture is a profession, an intellectual discipline, and an economic activity. In Latin America, it is also a reflection of social contrast. Outstanding Latin American practitioners of architecture and related disciplines here examine the current situation of their fields within that context. With respect to the development of architectural styles, the contributors show the intermingling of European colonial and indigenous influences, in which the past gives force to living tradition. Other chapters examine the nature of industrial design and the present and future roles architects may play in Latin American society.

CONTENTS

Civilization and Creativity: *D. Ribeiro* • Regional and Urban Influences as Limiting Factors on Latin American Architecture: *R. Segre* • The Present Significance of the Architecture of the Past: *G. Gasparini* • External Influences and the Significance of Tradition: *M. Cetto* • The Current Crisis in Latin American Architecture: *R. Vargas Salguero* and *R. López Rangel* • Industrial Design: An Ambiguous Reality: *G. Bonsiepe* • Technology: *E. Escobar Loret de Mola* • Meaning and Social Participation: *R. Segre*

216 pp. / bibliography, index / ISBN 0-8419-0532-0 /
1982   *$34.50*

HOLMES & MEIER PUBLISHERS, INC.
IUB Building
30 Irving Place, New York, N.Y. 10003

HANDBOOK OF LATIN AMERICAN ART

Comprehensive, Annotated Bibliography
1942–1980 in Three Volumes

Joyce W. Bailey, Director

This monumental new set—all three volumes of which are being published simultaneously—is the culmination of nearly a decade of planning and exhaustive scholarship.

Conceived as the first truly comprehensive and fully annotated "reference for the study of Latin American art wherever these traditions (ancient, colonial, modern) have existed over a period of time or do exist today in the Western Hemisphere," the *Handbook* merges the collaborative efforts of scores of individual scholars, 17 universities and scholarly institutions in North, South, and Central America, and a distinguished Board of Directors and its special advisors.

Totaling close to 3,000 pages, the three volumes present both bibliographic and text sections. The later comprise short introductory and theoretical essays in the three languages of the Americas—English, Spanish, and Portuguese. The bibliographic sections comprise some 15,000 title entries—in all cases briefly annotated. Cross-indices by subject, artist, and author are included in each volume, a total of approximately 8,000 index listings.

forthcoming 1983

AFRICA IN LATIN AMERICA

Edited by Manuel Moreno Fraginals
Translated by Leonor Blum

This UNESCO-sponsored volume continues and expands Holmes & Meier's ongoing series, *Latin America in Its Culture.*

It explores the rich and complex network of African influences on Latin American languages, religion, customs, social organization, music, dance, art, and literature. It also brings the results of extensive scholarly researches to bear on the relationships among African and Latin American cultures. Indeed, in the view of at least one of the distinguished contributors (Octavio Ianni), the forced introduction of Africans as slaves in Latin America resulted in the creation of a virtual "new race" whose unique consciousness has belatedly come to the fore, socially and politically, in our time.

The contributors and their subjects include: Octavio Ianni on Social Organization and Alienation; Richard Allsopp on African Influences on Language in the Caribbean; Edward Kamau Braithwaite on the African Presence in Literature of the Caribbean; Odilio Urfe on Music and Dance in Cuba; Isabel Aretz on Music and Dance in Latin America; Sidney Mintz on the Africa of Latin America; and Jean Casimir on Slavery and Colonization in Haiti.

ca 400 pp./bibliography, index/ISBN 0-8419-0748-X/
forthcoming 1983 $39.50

HOLMES & MEIER PUBLISHERS, INC.
IUB Building
30 Irving Place, New York, N.Y. 10003